CONTENTS

ACKNOWLEDGEMENTS

This study was funded by the National Council for Curriculum and Assessment (NCCA) and the Gender Equality Unit of the Department of Education and Science, which was established under the National Development Plan (2000-2006) and co-funded by European Structural Funds. We are particularly grateful to Anne Looney, Peter Johnson, Rhona McSweeney and Maureen Bohan for their extremely helpful support and assistance during the course of the research. The study also benefited from discussions of preliminary findings with the Junior Cycle Review Committee and the Council of the NCCA.

As always, the study would not have been possible without the ongoing assistance of school principals, teachers and students. We would like to express our sincere gratitude for the time and effort invested by the case-study schools in the research process.

Within the ESRI, we are very grateful to staff in the Survey Unit, particularly James Williams, Fergal Rhatigan and Pauline Needham, for organising the survey of students. James Williams was an invaluable source of advice and help in designing the study as a whole and the student questionnaire in particular. Helpful comments on earlier drafts of the study were given by our colleagues, Philip O'Connell, Fran McGinnity, Yvonne McCarthy, Richard Layte and Brendan Whelan. We are very grateful to Patricia Byrne for the administrative support she provided throughout the course of the study. Pat Hopkins is to be thanked for her, as always, cheerful and efficient production of copies of the many drafts of the book.

Any remaining errors or omissions are the sole responsibility of the authors.

LIST OF TABLES

LIST OF FIGURES

Chapter One

INTRODUCTION AND METHODOLOGY

This book looks at the experiences of students in the second year of the junior cycle. It has two main aims: firstly, to capture the 'student voice' in looking at key aspects of the student experience of teaching, learning and organisation of the curriculum in schools; and secondly, to explore changes in student attitudes to school and schoolwork over the course of first and second year. The origins of this study lie in research conducted on the experiences of students making the transition into post-primary education (Smyth et al., 2004). The *Moving Up* study drew on the perspectives of the key stake-holders, namely school management, teachers, parents and students themselves across a range of case-study schools, in looking at factors influencing the transition process. It found that, while students encounter an array of different organisational and learning experiences in making the transition to post-primary education, only a minority of students experience sustained difficulties in adjusting to the new setting. It highlighted the ways in which schools could facilitate an easier transition for their students by providing more developed integration programmes in first year, providing a more positive school climate with good relations between teachers and students, facilitating a continuity of learning experiences by building upon the primary experience and allowing access to subjects with a practical focus. This book builds upon the *Moving Up* study to document the school experiences of students in their second year. The first section of this chapter places the study in the context of previous research on the 'student voice'. Section two describes the methodology used in the study while the third section outlines the structure of the book.

1.1 RESEARCH ON THE 'STUDENT VOICE'

1.1.1 The student voice and school improvement

International research-based literature on the importance of the student's voice in the context of schooling has grown rapidly in recent years. There seems to be an emerging consensus among researchers and educationalists that listening to students' voices provides useful insights into the issues that are important for students and can thus potentially contribute to school improvement (see Rudduck and Flutter, 2004a, 2004b; Flutter and Rudduck, 2004; Andersson, 1996; Wallace and Wildy, 1996; Jackson et al., 1998; Maden and Rudduck, 1997; Rudduck et al., 1996). It is argued that capturing the student voice can play an important role in education reform as it enables policy-makers to make school life more meaningful to students and informs opinions among school staff with regard to school development (Fletcher, 2003).

The 'student voice' has generally incorporated two distinct dimensions: firstly, the use of research or school self-evaluation to document the experiences and opinions of students in order to effect school improvement (an aspect which is discussed in the following section); and secondly, the extent to which students are formally involved in decision-making within the school. Traditionally in Western European societies, young people have been excluded from the processes of dialogue and decision-making within schools as well as in the educational system more generally; Rudduck and Flutter (2004a) argue that 'this bracketing out of [students'] voice is founded upon an outdated view of childhood which fails to acknowledge young people's capacity to take initiatives and to reflect on issues affecting their lives' (p. 1). This perspective has been reinforced by the view among school personnel that student involvement may 'lead to a dangerous place' (Macbeath et al., 2001) or 'anarchy' (Lynch, 1999). However, the level of involvement of students through structures such as student councils, prefect and student monitoring systems has increased in recent years, at least in the British context, as schools have discovered that such an approach may lead to improved student outcomes rather than being personally challenging for teachers or threatening to the institution (Macbeath et al., 2001; Thomas et al., 2000).

In spite of evidence of the spread of participatory structures within schools, student councils have been criticised for failing to actually give students a 'voice' in decision-making. Rudduck and Flutter (2004a) suggest that, in some cases, such measures may become, in effect, 'an extension of the surveillance structures' of the school (p. 17). Involvement in school councils is often viewed by students as a token gesture as they cannot influence major decisions made in the school, especially in terms of teaching and learning (Macbeath and Mortimore, 2001). In the Irish context, staff are often found to have a different perspective on student councils than students themselves, with teachers emphasising their consultative role while students were more likely to see councils as having a potential role in policy formulation (Keogh and Whyte, 2005). When students witness student councils as having no such influence in policy-making within the school, they tend not to take them seriously (Lynch, 1999). It has also been suggested that participatory structures may focus on particular groups of students to the exclusion of others; Holdsworth and Thomson (2001) argue that the existing approach to student involvement depends on the existence of an 'ideal student . . . who likes school, negotiates, resolves conflicts, manages their own learning and constructs knowledge. Students who have 'a voice' are well behaved. Calling out, yelling out or walking out do not . . . constitute 'voice'. Students are expected to have one voice and one youth culture' (p. 243).

Nevertheless, it could be argued that student involvement can facilitate schools taking account of the unique perspective of young people and can improve our understanding of students' experiences of schooling and learning: 'it is important to know what pupils think will make a difference to their commitment to learning and, in turn, to their progress and achievement' (Rudduck and Flutter, 2004a, p. 2). Similarly, Sammons et al. (2004) and Gray et al. (1999) argue that schools could benefit from taking into account students' perspectives and giving them more prominent roles. A similar sentiment is voiced in the Irish context by Devine (2004) who suggests that, considering the amount of time spent by children in school, students should be consulted in the issues that are important to them. The importance of consulting with children in relation to issues shaping their lives is also strongly emphasised in the National Children's Strategy (2002).

1.1.2 The student voice and teaching and learning

One of the areas where schools are seen as benefiting from consultation with students is in relation to learning. Rudduck (2002) suggests a number of benefits arising from dialogue between teachers and students. For students, being able to put forward their views and having them taken seriously would give them a stronger sense of membership so that they feel positive about the school; a stronger sense of respect and self-worth so that they feel positive about themselves; and, a stronger sense of the self-as-learner so that they see becoming involved in school as worthwhile and contributing to the improvement of teaching and learning. On the other hand, teachers can gain a more open perception of young people's capabilities; the capability to see the familiar from a different angle; a readiness to change thinking and practice in the light of these perceptions; a renewed sense of excitement in teaching; and a practical agenda for improvement (p. 127).

Research in the British context has indicated that, when students are encouraged to reflect on their experiences and express their views, most do so accurately; they can readily identify things that affect their learning and concentration and such information can feed directly into school planning and development (Thomas et al., 2000; Rudduck and Flutter, 2004a). Furthermore, students can highlight issues which are not considered as important by teachers. Thus, Macbeath et al. (2001) highlight a mismatch between teachers' and pupils' perceptions with regard to school experiences, for example, in the appropriate form of assessment to be used. Similarly, in one pilot project teachers were positive about students remaining in the same base classes for all of their subjects while students saw this as an impediment to mixing with other students (Hargreaves, 1996). A study by Duffield et al. (2000), focusing on the experiences of 13-14 year old students, showed that school staff and students have very different views of the learning process. Teachers focused on achievement as a core goal but young people viewed the attainment of good grades instrumentally and were disengaged from the learning process in any substantive sense. In this way, acknowledging students' voice in the classroom means acknowledging their active role in the learning process (Kordalewski, 1999).

Researchers have emphasised that recognising student perspectives on teaching and learning will only lead to change if power issues within a school are identified and if the student's voice is given legitimacy. Fielding (2004) thus stressed the lack of 'space' where staff and students can address each other as equals, given a context where school staff have greater power within existing structures. In other words, only by promoting equality and finding 'spaces' in which students can exercise their voices will a transformation take place. It is also important to remember that power issues are already present among students in terms of whose voice is being heard. Some researchers note that 'status [is] often rooted in competence in talk, which may, in turn, be linked, to social class differences. There are many silent or silenced voices – pupils who would like to say things about teaching and learning but who don't feel able to without a framework that legitimates comment and provides reassurance that teachers will welcome their comments and not retaliate' (Thomas et al., 2000, p. 131). At the same time, students are seen as having a lot to contribute in terms of teaching and learning and as contributing to changing schools into more effective educational environments where a positive learning culture prevails – 'where pupils and teachers feel that it is "cool to learn"' (Osborn, 2001, p. 277).

1.1.3 Students in the 'middle years'

Depending on the nature of different educational systems across countries, certain school years can be seen as having a strong 'identity'. The first year of post-primary education usually involves major changes in experiences for students in terms of exposure to different teaching methods, school subjects and school climate (Eccles et al., 1993; Galton et al., 2003; O'Brien, 2004; Smyth et al., 2004). Examination years also have a distinct identity. The end of lower secondary schooling is usually characterised by a heightened focus on academic achievement and preparation for exams. For some students this stage also marks the end of formal schooling. Increased academic pressure also characterises the end of upper secondary schooling as formal exam results often influence a young person's educational and career outcomes. In contrast, the 'middle year' in lower secondary education and the early part of upper secondary edu-

cation may be more difficult to characterise and these stages have sometimes been referred to as 'back burner' years.

In Britain, Doddington et al. (1999) observed that students' engagement with school tends to peak in years when they are actively involved
in subject choice (years 7 and 11). However, some students experience
problems with motivation and engagement, and hence, with performance
towards the end of year 7 that will last all the way through year 8 and, in
some cases, into year 9. Elsewhere, the British researchers Harris and
Rudduck (1993) note that, while students are sufficiently challenged in
the first year of secondary school, the situation is very different in their
second year as students have got used to the new environment. Being
integrated into the new school coupled with not having to prepare for
State exams was seen as contributing to students feeling more relaxed
about learning and thus a decline in academic performance.

Doddington et al. (1999) argue that many pupils do not realise the
importance of sustaining continuity in learning. The 'middle year' is
generally not considered to be an important year. They note that students' attitudes may also be influenced by staffing policies whereby better teachers are likely to be assigned to the exam years and only modest
attention is given to those who teach the 'middle years'. The authors argue that students need to be challenged at the end of the first year in secondary school; otherwise their attention is likely to turn away from
schoolwork to peer-related issues. Rudduck and Flutter (2004a) suggest
that using student voice in exploring perspectives during the 'middle'
years could provide valuable insights into students' perceptions and
would help schools to come up with ways of maintaining students' interest and avoiding disengagement. Student disengagement at this stage
may be reinforced by school structures, in particular by the greater
prevalence of ability grouping practices in the 'middle year' with some
students feeling they are less valued as learners than others.

Developmental changes occurring as a result of adolescence may
also contribute to changes in students' attitudes to, and performance in,
their schoolwork. It is generally agreed that early adolescence can be
characterised as a time of socio-cognitive development when young people develop a sense of autonomy, independence, social interaction and
self-determination (Urdan et al., 1995; Lee et al., 1983). A desire for

greater independence and an increased involvement in non-academic activities and with peers during the middle grades has been well documented (Hargreaves, 1996; Erikson, 1968; Anderman and Maehr, 1994; Wenz-Gross and Siperstein, 1998; Cotterell, 1996; Goodenow, 1993). Hence, the middle years become a 'time of tension between the pull of the peer group and the demands of work in classrooms' (Doddington et al., 1999, p. 32). As other areas take precedence over learning, a dip in motivation and academic achievement may be observed as students react to the mismatch between the traditional school environment and their growing sense of adulthood (Doddington et al., 1999; Anderman and Maehr, 1994). This mismatch can often result in disengagement, underachievement and sometimes early school leaving (Kroeger et al., 2004; Goodenow, 1993).

Research suggests that, in order to maintain students' motivation and interest in school, it is important to ensure that learning is seen as a continuous experience throughout the various years and not just as relating to tests and examinations. In addition, students in their middle years wish to be treated as adults whose opinions are respected, who are given enough responsibility and who are adequately challenged as well as supported by the staff (Rudduck, 2002). Rudduck argues that if these 'conditions of learning' are not met, students are likely to let their learning drift, a pattern which is most likely in years without a specific identity (such as the second year in secondary education): 'Year 8 seems to lack the kind of identity and challenge that engages students and, as a consequence, there can be among those whose motivation is fragile, a turning away from learning' (p. 125). She warns that this 'drifting' in year 8 can have longer-term implications for students' later schooling careers.

1.1.4 Research in the Irish context

In keeping with research in other Western countries, studies in the Irish context have emphasised the hierarchical nature of school organisations both at primary and post-primary levels. Devine (2004) documents the difference in status between students and adults in the primary school and the lack of consultation with students concerning key issues within the school relating to curriculum, pedagogy and assessment. She argues for the importance of listening to students' own views in looking at school change, especially given the capacity of (even young) students 'to reflect both critically and constructively on what happens to them in school' (2004, p. 124). Similarly, Lynch and Lodge (2002) indicate that the exercise of power and authority is a major concern among young people in post-primary schools and that students themselves wish for a greater democraticisation of schooling, both at the organisational and classroom levels.

A number of other research studies have sought to capture the 'student voice', looking at student experiences of the transition to post-primary education (O'Brien, 2004; Smyth et al., 2004), views of specific subjects such as Mathematics (Lyons et al., 2003) and experiences of particular programmes such as Transition Year (Smyth et al., 2004), often placing student accounts in the context of the views of other stakeholders such as school principals, teachers and parents. Research in the Irish context has tended to focus on 'key' school years, such as the first year of post-primary school (O'Brien, 2004; Smyth et al., 2004) and the examination years (Hannan et al., 1996; Smyth, 1999) or have looked at students across a range of years (see, for example, Lynch and Lodge, 2002). Students in the 'middle years' have thus been relatively neglected in Irish research. The PISA studies (see, for example, Shiel et al., 2001) include many second year students but as students are sampled on the basis of 'age' rather than 'stage', they cannot give a holistic overview of experiences among second year students. The book by Lyons et al. (2003) is one of the few studies looking specifically at second year students, focusing on student experiences of teaching and learning in Mathematics.

This study seeks to build upon existing research and use the 'student voice' as a tool in exploring second year students' experiences in terms of their perceptions of school in general and teaching and learning issues in particular. It is hypothesised that students in second year will resemble those analysed in other 'middle years' research internationally as they are mid-way through the three-year lower secondary programme. An innovative aspect of the study is its longitudinal nature, allowing us to explore changes in student attitudes and perceptions over the first two years of post-primary schooling. The way in which the study was carried out is discussed in the following section.

1.2 METHODOLOGY

The main research questions addressed in this study are:

- To what extent do students' attitudes to school change as they move from first to second year within the junior cycle?

- Are certain types of schools more successful at maintaining student engagement with the learning process?

- Do certain groups of students (in terms of gender, social class background and ability group) experience greater disengagement from school over time?

- What teaching methods and classroom contexts do students see as facilitating their learning?

- What is the quality of interaction between teachers and students, and among students themselves, in second year?

In keeping with international research (see, for example, Doddington et al., 1999), it is hypothesised that students will have more negative attitudes to school in second year than in their first year of post-primary education. However, it is anticipated that the extent to which student attitudes change will vary across different groups of students and different school contexts. It is hypothesised that students allocated to lower stream classes will experience greater disengagement with the learning process over time, in line with the patterns evident in first year (Smyth et al., 2004). At the school level, it is expected that more developed support structures for students will help prevent student disengagement, especially if they are underpinned by a positive informal climate within the school. Because of the emphasis in this study on documenting the 'student voice', no prior assumptions are made about the kinds of teaching approaches which will facilitate student learning but rather the study will explore students' own views on teaching and learning.

The study is located within the 'mixed methods' tradition, using both quantitative and qualitative research methods. 'Mixed methods' research has become increasingly prevalent in social and educational research (Tashakorri and Teddlie, 2003). Such approaches allow researchers to study different aspects of the reality under investigation and thus increase the amount and range of evidence available to them (Gorard and Taylor, 2004). Many of the most influential studies of school effects have employed case-studies of schools, often in conjunction with representative surveys of schools. Some researchers have used a purposive sample of schools designed to capture a wide variety of school characteristics (see, for example, Rutter et al., 1979; Smith and Tomlinson, 1989). Others have selected schools to capture key dimensions hypothesised to influence student experiences and outcomes. Thus, in the Louisiana School Effectiveness Study, Teddlie and Stringfield (1993) used survey data to select 18 schools in terms of their effectiveness and socio-economic composition for longitudinal study (see also earlier work by Brookover et al., 1979).

Sample selection

Table 1.1: Sample of case-study schools

Subject Choice		Student Integration in First Year	
		Less Emphasis	*Stronger Emphasis*
Early	Mixed ability	Barrack St Wattle St.	Dawson St.
	Streamed/banded	Park St. Hay St.	Dawes Point
Later (taster)	Mixed ability	Harris St.	Fig Lane Belmore St.
	Streamed/banded	Dixon St.	Lang St. Argyle St.

Note: Pseudonyms are used to identify the schools.

As part of the *Moving Up* study, a postal survey of all post-primary principals was conducted to explore school practices in relation to junior cycle provision. On the basis of this survey, a purposive sample of twelve case-study schools was selected in terms of the school's approach to integrating first year students into the school, the school's approach to subject choice and the approach to ability grouping, dimensions which were expected to play an important role in shaping student integration and learning over the course of first year and beyond (see Smyth et al., 2004). Such an approach allows us to locate detailed case-studies of organisation and process within twelve schools in the context of national policy and practice within post-primary schools.

The sample of schools is outlined in Table 1.1. Firstly, it included six schools which used streaming, that is, allocated students by 'ability' to their base classes, and six which used mixed ability allocation, with students being allocated randomly to their classes. Secondly, six of the schools required students to select their subjects on or before entry to the school while the remainder allowed students to 'sample' their subjects for part or all of first year before making their choice. Thirdly, six schools which appeared from the postal survey responses to have a strong emphasis on student integration were selected along with six which had less of an emphasis on such practices. When more detailed information was gathered from the case-study schools, it was evident that three of the schools (Dixon St., Wattle St. and Harris St.) had a stronger emphasis on student integration than was apparent from the postal survey responses. These schools can therefore be regarded as closer to the 'stronger emphasis' schools in terms of their policy and practice.

Table 1.2: Profile of the case-study schools

School	Size	Sector	Social Mix
Dawson St.	Medium	Community/comprehensive	Mixed
Lang St.	Small	Vocational	Working-class; disadvantaged
Barrack St.	Small	Girls' secondary	Working-class; disadvantaged
Dixon St.	Large	Vocational	Working-class; disadvantaged
Park St.	Large	Boys' secondary	Mixed
Hay St.	Small	Vocational	Working-class
Fig Lane	Large	Coeducational secondary (fee-paying)	Middle-class
Argyle St.	Large	Community/comprehensive	Mixed
Harris St.	Large	Girls' secondary	Middle-class
Dawes Point	Small	Boys' secondary	Working-class; disadvantaged
Belmore St.	Large	Girls' secondary	Mixed
Wattle St.	Small	Boys' secondary	Mixed; disadvantaged

Two of the twelve case-study schools discontinued their involvement in the study between first and second year. In order to capture diversity across different school contexts, two additional schools were asked to participate in the second year of the study. These schools were chosen in line with the three dimensions originally used to select the schools for the study of first year students. Because these two schools were not included in the first year part of the study, they are not included in all tables and graphs, especially those in Chapter Six.

The profile of the case-study schools, including the 'new' schools, is presented in Table 1.2. The schools vary in terms of sector, size, location and designated disadvantaged status. In order to provide contextual information on the schools throughout the remainder of the book, abbreviations will be used: 'gs' will refer to a girls' school, 'bs' to a boys' school, 'cd' to a coeducational school, 'wc' to a school with a working-class student profile, 'mc' to a school with a middle-class student profile and 'mxc' to a school with a mixed social class intake. Thus, 'gs mc' will indicate a girls' school with a middle-class student intake.

Case-studies of Schools

Within each of the twelve case-study schools, information was collected from second year students and from the key personnel who had responsibility for this year group. Using information from both students and school personnel allows us to build up a more complete picture of school policy and process, while still retaining the 'student voice' as a key focus.

Like all research, this study has some limitations. Students at this stage are experiencing a range of psychological and physiological changes which impact on their life experiences (see Erikson, 1968; Cotterell, 1996). A holistic analysis of young people's experiences would require an analysis of their family life and their neighbourhood context along with their peer relations outside school. However, the focus of this study is on young people's experiences in one, albeit very important, aspect of their lives, that of school. For this reason, interviews were conducted with second year students and the key personnel dealing with them rather than with their parents and wider social circle. Given the crucial role school occupies in the lives of young people and the long-term implications of educational 'success' for adult life, a focus on school experiences is seen as a relevant one.

Within each school, self-completion questionnaires were administered to all second year students in March 2004. These questionnaires covered student attitudes to school and subjects, their views on teaching and learning, their perspective on equality issues within the school, and their aspirations for the future. Analyses are based on questionnaires completed by 905 students making up 86 per cent of all second year students in the case-study schools. Matching information on the ten schools which participated in both the first and second year of the study yields information on 665 students for longitudinal analysis. In order to more fully capture the 'student voice', group interviews were carried out by two members of the project team with second year students in March 2004. Within each school, a group of six students from each class was selected at random by the project team from the list of second year students in the school and students were interviewed within their base class groups. A total of 47 group interviews were conducted in the case-study schools. These interviews focused on students' experiences of being in second year, their views on effective teaching and what helps them learn, their views on tests and exams and their perceptions of school climate. These interviews were recorded and transcribed; transcripts were analysed using the QSR N6 package in order to identify the central themes emerging from the interviews. Quotes from the student interviews are used in Chapters Four and Five in order to illustrate the key themes emerging from the student interviews in the words of students themselves.

Using information from both questionnaires and group interviews allows us to utilise the relative strengths of each approach. The questionnaires allow us to capture variation between individual students in their attitudes to school and their subjects; this information can be compared with that gathered in first year to look at the way in which individual students change and develop as they move through school. Questionnaires also have an advantage in providing greater privacy to the student; a student may be more willing to admit to having been bullied in a self-completion questionnaire than they might in a group setting, for example. However, questionnaires have some disadvantages. Their structured nature means that students can only respond in relation to issues that the researchers deem important rather than ones which they themselves feel shape their school experiences. Furthermore, it may be difficult to explore complex issues, such as what aspects of teaching enhance learning, in a very structured way. In contrast, focus group interviews allow students to raise issues which are of concern to them and these issues can be followed up by the interviewer. They can also help researchers to better understand and explain patterns revealed in the survey data (Morgan, 1996; Johnson and Turner, 2003). However, group interviews must be handled carefully since they may become dominated by one or two individuals and students may be wary of expressing some views in front of their classmates. For these reasons, questionnaire and group interview data provide complementary perspectives on the student experience in second year.

While the focus of the study was on documenting student perspectives of school, it was considered vital to place their accounts within the context of the perspectives of key personnel within the school. As a result, in-depth interviews were carried out with the key staff members dealing with second year students, namely, the school principal, the year head for second year and the class tutors. These interviews focused on (perceptions of) support and learning structures for second year students in the case-study schools. In order to preserve the anonymity of the respondents, the type of post held is not specified in the analyses. A total of 65 interviews were conducted with key personnel in the case-study schools. These interviews were recorded and transcribed; transcripts were analysed using the QSR N6 package.

The data gathered were used in two distinct ways: firstly, information on the twelve case-study schools was used to provide a 'snap-shot' of the views of second year students; and secondly, information collected from the ten schools that had participated in both phases of the study was used to explore changes in attitudes among students between first and second year. The use of both quantitative information (from the student questionnaire) along with qualitative information (from the student interviews) allows us to provide a more complete picture of students' own experiences of moving through the junior cycle.

1.3 OUTLINE OF THE BOOK

Chapters Two and Three draw on in-depth interviews with key personnel in the case-study schools to set the scene by documenting provision for second year students. Chapter Two focuses on the support structures in place for the students while Chapter Three examines learning structures, including approaches to ability grouping, subject choice and learning support provision. These chapters provide vital contextual information for understanding the different experiences of second year student documented in Chapters Four to Six. Chapters Four and Five provide a 'snap-shot' of the views of second year students in the case-study schools. Chapter Four looks at the school climate from the perspective of students in terms of their interaction with teachers and with other students. Chapter Five examines student perspectives on what makes an effective teacher and what helps them to learn; student views on home-work and assessment are also explored. Chapter Six draws on the longi-tudinal part of the study to analyse the extent to which student attitudes to school change between first and second year and to identify the factors which influence such changes. Chapter Seven summarises the main find-ings of the study and highlights some issues for policy development.

Chapter Two

SUPPORT STRUCTURES FOR SECOND YEAR STUDENTS IN THE CASE-STUDY SCHOOLS

This chapter draws on interviews conducted with key personnel dealing with second year students in each of the case-study schools; those interviewed included the Principal, Year Head, Class Tutors and Guidance Counsellors. The information that was gathered from those involved with second year students provides us with an overview of supports for the year group, the perceived efficacy of these supports in dealing with issues that arise up with second years, disciplinary structures in the schools and how key personnel in the schools view second year students as a group. The nature of the support structures within schools may be particularly important in light of the decline in student motivation in the 'middle years' identified in pervious research (see Chapter One). The first section of this chapter outlines the nature of support structures for second year students in the case-study schools while the second section examines staff perceptions regarding the adequacy of these structures. Section three looks at anti-bullying policies within the schools while the fourth section examines more general discipline policy. The fifth section analyses the identity of second year students from the perspective of key personnel.

2.1 MAIN SUPPORT STRUCTURES

There are common support structures in place for second year students across the twelve case-study schools. However, the extent to which these supports are structured varies greatly across schools as does staff satisfaction with these supports. All of the case-study schools rely on the

Class Tutor/Year Head support system and deem this the main support for second year students. However, many schools also involve other personnel in providing support to second year students, mainly the Guidance Counsellor or chaplain, and, in some cases, a matron, student councillors or the Home-School Liaison Co-ordinator. Seven of the schools (Argyle Street, Dawson Street, Harris Street, Dixon Street, Park Street, Dawes Point and Wattle Street) mentioned that the Guidance Counsellor is involved in offering support to second year students with three schools (Dawson Street, Dixon Street and Fig Lane) also mentioning a school chaplain. The majority of the schools had student councils in place which were intended to represent the views of students in the school (see Table 2.1). However, in all but one school, these student councillors had no particular brief to deal with second year students. Harris Street school, a girls' school, was unique in having student councillors who adopted a mentoring role with second year students, an approach which followed on from the use of student mentors with first year students.

As well as varying in the personnel involved in providing support to second year students, the case-study schools differed in the extent to which such supports were formalised and formed an integrated structure within the school. On this basis, schools can be loosely classified as having strong or weak formalised support structures for second year students (Table 2.1). Those schools with stronger and more integrated supports are Dawson Street, Dixon Street, Dawes Point, Belmore Street, Park Street, Hay Street and Harris Street. Conversely, Barrack Street, Fig Lane, Lang Street, Wattle Street and Argyle Street appear to have somewhat less extensive supports. Among the case-study schools, smaller schools appear less likely to have strongly formalised support structures. This may indicate that small school size facilitates greater *informal* contact among staff and between staff and students; the extent to which informal contact can compensate for lack of formal support structures is explored further in Chapter Four.

Table 2.1: Supports for second year students

	Formalised support structures for second year students	Main Support	Guidance Counsellor mentioned	Student Council	Other supports mentioned	Social mix[1]	Gender profile	School size
Dawson Street	Strong	Class Tutor/Year Head	Yes	Yes	Chaplain, NEPS	Mixed	Coed	Medium
Dixon Street	Strong	Class Tutor/Year Head	Yes	Yes	Chaplain	Working class	Coed	Large
Park Street	Strong	Class Tutor/Year Head	Yes	Yes	NEPS	Mixed	Boys	Large
Hay Street	Strong	Class Tutor/Year Head	Yes	Yes	NEPS, HSLC	Working class	Coed (mostly boys)	Small
Harris St.	Strong	Class Tutor/Year Head	Yes	Yes	NEPS	Middle class	Girls	Large
Dawes Point	Strong	Class Tutor/Year Head	No	Yes	NEPS	Working class	Boys	Small

	Formalised support structures for second year students	Main Support	Guidance Counsellor mentioned	Student Council	Other supports mentioned	Social mix[1]	Gender profile	School size
Belmore Street	Strong	Class Tutor/Year Head	No	Yes	Counsellor for students	Mixed	Girls	Large
Barrack Street	Weak	Class Tutor/Year Head	No	Yes		Working class	Girls	Small
Fig Lane	Weak	Class Tutor/Year Head	Yes	Yes		Middle class	Coed	Large
Argyle St.	Weak	Class Tutor/Year Head	No	No		Mixed	Coed	Large
Lang Street	Weak	Class Tutor/Year Head	No	No		Working class	Boys	Small
Wattle Street	Weak	Class Tutor/Year Head	No	Yes		Mixed	Boys	Small

Note: 1. Social mix was based on disadvantaged status as designated by the Department of Education and Science in conjunction with the social profile of the student cohort.

The extent to which formalised support structures represent a continuation of support for first year students varies across schools (see Table 2.2). In five of the schools, such a continuation of strong student support from one year to the next is evident. However, four of the schools had a number of measures to promote student integration in first year whereas support was less developed for students in second year. In two of the schools (Park St. and Hay St.), comparatively little emphasis had been placed on student integration in first year but a formalised system for supporting students was apparent in second year. One school, Barrack St., had relatively underdeveloped formal support structures for students in the two year groups; however, it may be the case that the small size of the school allowed for greater informal interaction among school personnel and students.

Table 2.2: Relationship between support structures in first and second year

		Formalised support structures in second year	
		Strong	Weak
Emphasis on student integration in first year	Strong	Belmore St. Dawson St. Dixon St. Harris St. Dawes Point	Fig Lane Argyle St. Lang St. Wattle St.
	Weak	Park St. Hay St.	Barrack St.

The following section explores in greater depth the different school practices utilised in the twelve case-study schools in offering support to second year students. This is followed by an examination of the extent to which key personnel are satisfied with current provision and what structures they would like to see in place for their students.

2.1.1 Role of the Year Head and Class Tutor

In most of the case-study schools, the role of the Year Head centred on discipline, including monitoring student attendance. Other aspects of their role included administration and pastoral care of students. In many cases, the role was multi-faceted, combining a number of these functions. The Year Head in Harris St. school, a school with strong formal structures, illustrated the range of activities included in the role:

> Well to deal with any problems that any of the Second Years [have], to ensure the smooth running of the year, to organize their subject choices, to deal with any problems — discipline or otherwise — that they may have and to see that they get whatever help they need. What else? In charge in particular of coordinating information to the form teachers and holding a meeting of the form teachers on a regular basis and coordinating with them about different activities. (Harris St. School, gs mc).

Compared to the Class Tutors, Year Heads generally had less direct contact with the students. Issues, particularly discipline issues, were referred to them by the Class Tutors or subject teachers:

> Mostly it's people coming knocking on my door and they'll usually have a teacher attached to them, sort of saying this guy just won't behave himself and my job is mainly on the punitive side . . . So it's mainly that, keeping a check on the attendance obviously as well . . . So I'd be tracking attendance, looking at their behaviour, that they have their uniforms. (Hay St. School, cd wc).

Year Heads were also more likely than Class Tutors to have contact with parents, mainly in relation to discipline issues (see section 2.4 below).

The role of the Class Tutor tended to focus on three main aspects: administration/organisational issues (including student registration), pastoral care for students and discipline. These roles are not mutually exclusive with many Class Tutors incorporating all of these strands in their day to day work. One quote from a Class Tutor in Dawson St. school indicates the diverse range of activities involved and the flexibility required from Class Tutors:

> Well, first of all every morning I would take the registration for the group and I would take in notes if they were absent and check their notes on why they were absent and reasons like that. And then any notices that are to be given out on a daily basis to the tutor group, I give those out at registration. I check uniforms and I check their journals to make sure they're signed. Then if the students have any

issues or any problems themselves they would come to me and I would deal with those, for example bullying or just anything in general that's annoying them or anything like that. And then also if a teacher has given me an incident form regarding a student and discipline in a class I would also have to deal with that and then pass that on to the year head. (Dawson St. School, cd mxc).

The most frequently mentioned aspect of the Class Tutor's role across the case-study schools was discipline:

First thing is checking the journals in the morning and make sure they have a full uniform on. If they have been off that they have notes, if they were in trouble with a teacher then I take it to the next level, check to see if they have their punishment work done. Contact with parents, them ringing me if there is any problem, meeting parents. (Dixon St. School, cd wc).

The next most frequently mentioned aspect of the tutor role was providing support for students in their class group. Several of the tutors spoke about dealing with problems among their second year students, although their reference to dealing with student problems was often ambiguous and did not clearly specify whether they dealt with personal problems, behavioural problems or academic problems:

If they have a particular individual problem, they're supposed to come to you about it. (Dawes Point School, bs wc)

The extent to which students did actually approach tutors in relation to specific problems is discussed further in section 2.1.5 below.

Variation was evident across the case-study schools in how the role of the tutor was defined, with some schools placing a greater emphasis on the disciplinary function of the tutor than others. However, Class Tutors within the same schools were also found to differ in how they interpreted their role with some emphasising the discipline aspects while others viewed their role as pastoral in nature. Only in one school, Dawes Point, did the tutors consistently define their role as monitoring attendance.

2.1.2 The Class Tutor/Year Head system

The most commonly mentioned support structure across schools is the Class Tutor/Year Head system. Most class tutors are seen as the first port of call for students and would generally have the most contact with the students on a day-to-day basis:

> I think that there is a genuine reliance and with good reason on the structure there say with the year head and class teachers. There is a good relationship in general between teachers and students in the school. (Argyle St. School, cd mxc).

In trying to offer support to students, Class Tutors regularly liaise with the Year Head. In turn, Year Heads often involve the Guidance Counsellor or the Home School Liaison Co-ordinator if they feel it is necessary:

> Well I think the class tutor would be the first level, so hopefully they [students] will have developed a relationship with their class tutor . . . and then you have the year head obviously as well can get involved, so we've a chaplain here as well so . . . I would say there's generally a fairly good pastoral system in the school. (Fig Lane, cd mc).

There was some variation across the case-study schools, however, in the time allocated for co-ordination between Class Tutors and Year Heads regarding student welfare. In some schools, such as Dawes Point and Belmore St., specific time was allocated for key personnel to meet regarding students:

> [We have] a weekly meeting, whereby the class teachers sit down with the year head and identify problems or difficulties and that's been hugely beneficial. It's thrown up problems very quickly with the result that they're being identified and dealt with whether it be academic, whether it be learning needs, whether it be you know contacting parents or whatever and then the home school liaison kicks in. (Dawes Point School, bs wc).

However, in other cases contact between Class Tutors and other personnel was largely informal:

> It's pretty informal but that's the way the school works, we all know each other on a one to one basis anyway. (Fig Lane School, cd mc)

2.1.3 Other support structures for second year students

Many of the schools have other supports as well as the Class Tutor/Year Head system. In seven of the case-study schools, the Guidance Counsellor was seen as playing an important role in offering support to second year students who were experiencing particular problems. When Class Tutors or Year Heads felt they could not deal with a student's problem them-selves, they often referred the student on to the Guidance Counsellor:

> The counsellor of course, she's been great with some of them be-cause one or two of them have had major problems you know, that I felt were personal things, I felt I couldn't deal with it. I hadn't the expertise to do it. (Barrack St. School, gs wc).

> I would have to say in fairness, I must say that our own career guid-ance teacher here is absolutely marvellous in terms of that you can refer people to him, in recent times now I would have had two stu-dents that I would have referred to him. (Dawes Point School, bs wc).

Additionally, some schools have a chaplain or a matron and their role is seen as vital in supporting the students with key personnel regularly mentioning them as someone the second years can go to with any prob-lem. In schools where they were present, they were often seen as the per-son the students found most approachable:

> In spite of them having a tutor who calls their name every morning and speaks to them every single morning of the week and a year head who is there on hand to meet with parents and so on all the time, the person that they felt most comfortable with was the chap-lain, we have an excellent chaplain. (Dawson St. School, cd mxc).

There is little evidence of other 'innovative' approaches used by the case-study schools in supporting second year students. However, an ad-ditional counsellor who worked with groups of students was available in Belmore Street and the Home-School-Community Liaison Co-ordinator was mentioned in Dawes Point. Several of the case-study schools had had student mentors in place to act as a support for first year students (Smyth et al., 2004). However, this approach was not carried forward into second year. The exception was Harris St., where students appointed to the student council had a role in monitoring difficulties among, and providing support for, second year students. These student councillors were seen as being potentially more approachable for students, which was in keeping with perceptions of the student mentor system used for first year students in many schools (see Smyth et al., 2004):

> They have also like their task councillor, a Sixth Year, which I find invaluable because they will actually speak to her more than they'll actually speak to anyone else. (Harris St. School, gs mc).

2.1.4 Structure of supports

Most schools describe the supports they have in terms of individual supports. Although seven of the schools had more formalised support structures for second year students, only three schools had highly integrated structures where the supports closely linked into each other. In Harris St. and Dawes Point schools, there appears to be a ladder structure where the Class Tutor reports to the Year Head who then decides if they should seek further support from other key personnel such as the Guidance Counsellor or whether to refer students on to outside psychological services:

> The main [support], first of all the form teacher, they have also like their task councillor, a Sixth Year . . . and very often then I will sort of then make it known to the year head and then we would decide what . . . to do. Normally we would either, if it's quite serious, maybe contact the parents or guardians or whatever. If we thought it could be dealt with in the school we might maybe speak to [the guidance counsellors] and try and see what the problem is. (Harris St. School, gs mc).

> We meet every [week], . . . class tutors . . . and myself.

> Interviewer: And what kind of things would come up in those meetings?

> Everything would come up, basically what we do is we rotate [discussing] the classes . . . And then who we'd bring in there from time to time is the home school liaison officer or maybe the career guidance teacher or [a teacher] who is on special hours for students with difficulties, learning difficulties. . . . We do our best to pull all the strands together. (Dawes Point, bs wc)

Similarly, in Belmore Street, a pastoral care team was in place which met regularly to discuss issues arising with particular students and actions which could be taken to help them:

> Well I would be the first point of contact if there was something going on. But I would refer back to the pastoral care committee first, and then as a group they would decide what the next procedures would be, if they needed outside intervention or if it was necessary to get someone else or whatever involved. (Belmore St., gs mxc)

2.1.5 Willingness of students to talk to tutors

Although Class Tutors were seen as the first point of contact for second year students in the case-study schools, tutors differed in the extent to which they reported that students would actually approach them with problems. Many tutors felt that students would be reluctant to approach them to discuss personal matters:

> Interviewer: Would students ever tend to come to you to talk about personal problems or anything like that?
>
> Not really, I've never really been approached, maybe on one or two occasions but not ever from anybody who was within my tutor group, it would be maybe someone from another class who you just got on well with or who felt that they could trust you or something like that. (Park St., bs mxc)

Other tutors were more proactive in their approach and tried to identify students who may be having difficulties:

> Some of them wouldn't come up but you'd notice, meeting them every day and I teach them . . . as well as my tutor class, you'd notice a difference in their personality and you might just say it to them, "is everything ok?" or different things like that, but some of them would come up to you, a lot of them wouldn't. (Dawson St., cd mxc)
>
> I haven't had many cases of people coming directly with some particular problem but in general discussions with the class I might become aware of something like an element of bullying that's going on or something like that and then I would try to deal with that on their behalf. (Dawes Point, bs wc)

The role of the tutor in terms of discipline was seen as a potential barrier to students approaching teachers about problems:

> Normally I think the students are more comfortable going to them [guidance counsellors] rather than the form teacher. Because they probably see us in a discipline role as opposed to sort of pastoral care so they're slow to sort of discuss home problems. (Harris St., gs mc)

Having regular contact with the students in the form of class contact time or participation in non-academic activities was seen as facilitating a greater willingness on the part of students to discuss their problems:

> I would have one or two cases, very few, it wouldn't be a case of students would come to a teacher really, but they'd know probably in coming to me or we might be playing basketball or playing football with each other, they've no problem in actually mixing with me but I don't think they're great to discuss problems and I think the problems have to be very serious before they'd do so but never would a person come and say they'd problems at home. Now I don't know if they have problems, I don't know. (Park St., bs mxc)

> [Students don't come to me to] a great extent. But at the same time at the beginning of the term I put a lot of effort into team things that we could do together. And so that they could identify with each other and also with me as well. So like a few times they might have approached me in the corridor and said "Miss, we would like to talk to you". And they would stop and say can I come and see you. (Belmore St., gs mxc)

The individual personality of the tutor was also seen as playing a role in the degree of contact with students:

> It depends really on the personality of the form teacher, they're all very different and it depends, like some of the form teachers would be very involved in their class, others probably wouldn't. (Harris St., gs mc)

The extent to which students themselves are willing to approach teachers in relation to problems is discussed in Chapter Four below.

2.2 PERCEIVED ADEQUACY OF SUPPORT STRUCTURES FOR SECOND YEARS

Satisfaction with supports varies greatly between different schools. Although many schools say they are generally satisfied with their support structures, key personnel in all schools have some suggestions as to how supports for students can be improved (see Table 2.3). Satisfaction levels appear to be higher among staff in schools with mixed or more middle-class student intakes compared to those serving students from more disadvantaged backgrounds. There is no simple relationship between satisfaction with support structures and the extent to which such structures are formalised. Satisfaction levels are highest among key personnel in Belmore Street, which has highly integrated support structures in place, but also in Argyle Street and Fig Lane, which can be characterised as having less developed support systems for second year students.

Table 2.3: Main supports teachers would like to see for second years (which are not available currently)

Rank Order	Support	Main Schools Mentioning
1	More psychological support	Harris St, Park St, Lang St
2	More guidance services	Argyle St, Park St, Hay St
3	Improved contact with parents	Park St, Hay St
4	Time for teacher-student interaction/hours for class tutors	Dawson St, Harris St, Dawes Point
	Generally satisfied with supports	Fig Lane, Belmore St, Argyle St, Harris St, Dawes Point.

Schools reported three main inadequacies with the systems they have in place to support students (see Table 2.3). The single issue most frequently mentioned related to the perceived lack of psychological support services for students, an issue that has been raised in a national study of guidance services in post-primary schools (see McCoy et al., forthcoming). Key personnel expressed frustration at delays in getting students assessed and saw existing services, such as the National Educational

Psychological Service (NEPS), as having a narrow remit in not dealing with behavioural problems:

> I think the biggest problem is what's available to us outside school . . . in terms of . . . places to refer kids to, . . . for example for psychological assessment or educational assessment, or both, or say psychiatric services. . . . I can only go so far in my support with the kids and then I like to refer them on to other services outside school and really like it's very difficult to find those services. (Harris St. School, gs mc).

> The supports outside [the school] are pretty pathetic. The psychological service, it's all lip service. You could be waiting months. It's not acceptable when you need it now. (Park St. School, bs mxc).

> We've had some help now alright . . . from the NEPS, they have been quite good, . . . but it's not immediate . . . a week is a long time in their [students'] lives, they will have caused some difficulties in that time. (Lang St. School, bs wc).

In particular, key personnel would like improved external back-up and support in dealing with behavioural and other psychological issues among students:

> I think it would be a lot better if they [students] had someone specific that they could go to if they had a problem . . . if they had a problem you know, a qualified counsellor or whatever. (Harris St. School, gs mc).

A related issue raised by the key personnel was the need for more guidance hours or more Guidance Counsellors within the school in order to provide better support for students (see also McCoy et al., forthcoming):

> I mean in order to be able to intervene faster . . . one full-time counsellor for [the number of] pupils certainly could not be sufficient. So there will be a need for more counsellors. (Argyle St. School, cd mxc).

> I think certainly more guidance, personally, trained people who have counselling skills and who can deal with issues, there are certainly I think an increasing number of students, younger students suffering from depression for example. . . . So I think there's a lot of peer pressure on younger students and I think they have to be dealt with as well. It's very easy to kind of leave them go and not deal with it but more resources I think would be a huge factor. (Fig Lane School, cd mc).

A third issue raised by key personnel, especially in Park St. and Hay St. schools (schools with contrasting social profiles), related to the need for stronger links between the school and parents. Staff felt that a Home School Liaison Co-ordinator would be of great support to students and teachers as they considered that societal changes necessitate this service:

> I think every school should have a home school liaison officer, I think it shouldn't be just for the disadvantaged schools. . . . I think if you had that it might help to solve a lot of problems . . . because the reality is we've more and more students coming from either broken marriage or single parent relationships . . . I think if there was a back up of some sort, a non confrontational back up in terms of this home school liaison that it probably would be very advantageous. (Park St. School, bs mxc).

Where schools did have a Home School Liaison Co-ordinator, it was felt that extra time should be allocated to improve contact with parents and integrate them into the school's support structures:

> Maybe a better link up with the homes . . . When I say home school liaison person, they didn't teach, their job was to go out and to speak with the parents and try to advise the parents about programmes in the school and to give them that back up and that bit of encourage- ment and try to encourage the students. . . . That sort of service would be obviously wonderful if we had it . . . if you had somebody who had more time to call out, even though we do have somebody here that looks after home-school liaison, they wouldn't have that sort of time. (Hay St. School, cd wc).

Some key personnel also felt that the existing Class Tutor system had weaknesses and could not provide enough support to students due to its informal nature and the lack of time allocated to the role:

> Tutors tend to be the teachers who are on full-time teaching hours, teaching a large number of subjects, who would have a very, very heavy day to day workload, so really you're depending on the good will of a tutor to take on board the class that they have and work with them and it can work very well at times and at other times it can't and it's very difficult to put pressure on a teacher. (Dawson St. School, cd mxc).

> As a tutor, . . . if there was a specific time allocated for it, it might work a bit better than having it on a kind of an ad hoc basis. (Dawes Point, bs wc).

A number of key personnel in the case-study schools raised a more general issue about the appropriate role of teachers in the support structures of the school. Some teachers felt the line was increasingly being blurred between educating students and caring for the student's personal needs:

> Life is spilling more and more into school so teachers are now expected also to be social workers and psychologists and parents. (Harris St., gs mc).

This difficulty in defining the appropriate role of schools and teachers is summed up very well in the following extensive quotation:

> Interviewer: And are there any other support structures you'd like to see in place for junior cycle students?
>
> I think . . . it all depends on how I view what my job is. . . . If I'm an educator here, am I a social worker, am I a big brother, should I be concerned now that some of my students may be hungry? ... So like in looking at the support structures, I mean, like should schools get involved in the massive issue of alcohol abuse? Society has brought these things into the schools . . . when you say support structures, I'm just wondering you know, do I just walk in and teach my third year [subject] class? Teach the syllabus and that's my job in this school. And if I go beyond that, where does that end? Where does that end, how concerned should I be about kids who I know are getting absolutely no support at home, kids coming to school hungry, children who have absolutely no value whatsoever in education, parents who have no value . . . What is the function of schools? Where does education begin and end? And I have a syllabus to teach, I prepare students for exams, I certainly would be monitoring them obviously, you know, they are human beings, I'd be watching things but I think my brief on my watch has got so broad now that there's times I spend far more time dealing with issues. . . . If I was getting demoralised, it's because academically I've moved a far, far cry from what I trained to be. (Dawes Point School, bs wc).

A number of other more specific issues were raised by the key personnel in the case-study schools. These included the need for additional learning/academic support, personal development classes for students, a breakfast and lunch club, a homework club and training for staff in dealing with students' personal problems.

2.3 SUPPORT STRUCTURES TO DEAL WITH BULLYING

Bullying was raised as an issue by most of the key personnel dealing with second year students. Almost all schools mentioned having an anti-bullying policy in place although the approach taken varied across schools. Most staff considered that bullying was not a serious issue in their school, while recognising that they may have been unaware of the true levels of bullying among students:

> I wouldn't say it's a massive problem then again of course we only know what we hear. (Fig Lane School, cd mc).

> It's an issue, I'd be foolish to say it's not [a problem] . . . But I don't think we have a major, major bullying problem here. (Fig Lane School, cd mc).

In a few of the schools it was felt that bullying is more likely to occur amongst the junior cycle groups, particularly second year classes:

> It tends to, I think, erupt during second year going into third year with girls. It tends to happen more so with the junior school, at the junior end of the school. (Harris St. School, gs mc).

> Definitely second years for bullying and maybe in third year, those two groups are most likely. (Argyle St. School, cd mxc).

A number of key personnel in the schools feel that the isolation of a student by other students is a very common form of bullying. Some of the personnel are reluctant to label this behaviour as bullying but it is nonetheless recognised as a potential problem:

> There's quite a big group of friends in Second Year from all the different classes so they tend to keep together to the extent that it almost shuns other people away, you know, and you can consider that as bullying to a certain degree, ignoring people and things like that. (Harris St. School, gs mc).

Similarly, some key personnel felt that what the students defined as a bullying incident was not always bullying from the teacher's own perspective and this could lead to difficulties in tackling the issue:

> Really it is wrong to use the word [bullying] so often, and it's very bad for a child to allow a child to call something bullying when it is not. . . . But it is normal growing up problems and if you protect the child too much they never grow up. And they never learn as an adult how to cope when they are an adult with someone who is smart with them. (Belmore St. School, gs mxc).

> But bullying is not always as bullying appears, sometimes it's just somebody has isolated somebody, now that in a sense is bullying, but then sometimes [students] who feel they're being bullied make it out to be bigger than it actually is and you're trying to solve it on that basis. (Harris St. School, gs mc).

The key personnel in the case-study schools commonly voiced experiencing difficulties in tackling the issue of bullying. Some of the schools felt that they were doing their best but that bullying remained an issue in the school despite their efforts:

> Ultimately I feel that we are trapped because we have spoken to the children, we have had the workshop, the children have been spoken to individually, we have spoken to the groups. And when you are then in the situation whereby it's still going on, what do you do? (Harris St. School, gs mc).

> I think there will always be a certain amount of bullying going on in all years and it's always there and I think no matter [what] we can do it's always going to be there. (Fig Lane School, cd mc).

Most key personnel say they would discuss the issue with the students involved when they are made aware of a bullying incident. Sometimes other key personnel, such as the Guidance Counsellor or Principal, would then be consulted. Frequently key personnel inform a parent of the situation, particularly if it is seen as a serious incident:

> [The school] regards bullying as a serious matter . . . if I for example were aware that bullying was going on, I would inform the year head then and the principal. And we would interview . . . whatever students were involved and take it from there. Sometimes parents would

be informed if it were regarded as being serious enough. (Dawes Point, bs wc).

If a student comes to me or if a parent comes into this school and makes an allegation of bullying, I would investigate. First of all I would speak to the students in the class and maybe speak to the students that have been named as the perpetrators, to get to the bottom of the issue first of all . . . we have to find out exactly what's been happening. Sometime the home school liaison officer may have to go to speak to the parents at this stage, if the student has brought the problem to me I would involve the parents as well. Again then depending on the seriousness of the issue, I would involve the year head as well for second year and we might involve the parents of the person who was the alleged bully. (Lang St. School, bs wc).

Quite often an incident of bullying involves some kind of punishment for the bully involved:

All the students are spoken to and told what's acceptable, given whatever punishment, I suppose every situation is different but we try to deal with that straight away and stop it, stamp it out immediately, there's just a zero tolerance policy as regards bullying. (Park St. School, bs mxc)

It's automatic suspension if they bully people. (Barrack St. School, gs wc).

If it was a more serious incident, there's a three day suspension . . ., especially if it was any kind of physical bullying, three days' suspension just more or less there on the spot like you know. (Dawes Point School, bs wc).

Belmore Street School, a girls' school with highly integrated support structures for students, was the only school to talk about responding to the bully in a pastoral as well as a disciplinary sense:

You are suspended for bullying and the parents are sent for. . . . And we have our pastoral care committee and it deals with incidents where it definitely is bullying to try and to rehabilitate the person who is becoming the bully, as well as the discipline. (Belmore St. School, gs wc).

2.4 DISCIPLINE ISSUES

Most schools have a clear formal structure for dealing with discipline issues which arise among students. In most cases, incidents are recorded and, depending on the seriousness of the offence, some action would be taken. Commonly students have to engage in a certain number of breaches of discipline before significant action would be taken:

> The system of discipline in the school is that there is a mark system and if a subject teacher has a problem with a child, if they're not doing homework or if they haven't got their books or whatever, they might decide to give them a studies mark. If it's a very bad breach of discipline, for example bad language or something like that, they might give a conduct mark and there is a general mark if they're generally badly behaved, talking and inattentive or things like that. And if they get any combination of three marks in a week they get a detention. (Harris St. School, gs mc).

Normally the responsibility of enforcing the discipline code falls to the class tutor and/or the year head:

> It falls to the form teacher to check their discipline folders and different teachers fill in if they have misbehaved in class, mainly that's laughing and giggling . . . When a girl has, is it, three or four discipline entries, we have to have a discipline meeting, even if the Principal [was] already contacted, the Principal and the form teacher has to attend . . . a warning really, a letter home and further discipline entries then . . . it would come to suspension for three days. (Barrack St. School, gs wc).

> It's basically a five-stage system and if they get into trouble, depending on the seriousness of whatever has happened, they would be given either one stage, two stage, three stages depending. Normally just one stage would be given and once they reach five stages then it's expulsion at five stages, so they would have gone through this system and a culmination of stages. They would have gone through a system of obviously being talked to by myself, by the year head, by the principal, by the vice principal, parents would have been involved as much as possible, we try to get parents involved very early on so that they know what's going on as well as us and psychologists would have been involved as well where necessary. (Park St. School, bs mxc).

A number of key personnel reported that second year students were more likely to create discipline problems than first year students. Their behaviour was seen as more challenging and potentially disruptive (see section 2.5 below):

> They're inclined to come in late and that sort of thing, I mean you will invariably find second years will try the system more than first years, they get to know the ropes . . . they're a little bit more challenging in second year than they are in first year. (Hay St. School, cd wc).

> There definitely would be more discipline issues in second year than in first year. . . . They're intimidated by the older guys in first year, they feel they're the youngest in the school and maybe it's best to keep my head down and keep going. So a lot of discipline issues wouldn't arise in first year whereas by the time second year comes, there's a lot of maturing going on there, a lot of hormonal changes in the boys definitely, there would definitely be more discipline issues. (Lang St. School, bs wc).

> Second year would be giving backchat to teachers, the second and third years and by the middle of the third year they are over it usually. (Belmore St. School, gs mxc).

Staff in the streamed schools tended to report more discipline issues with lower stream than with higher stream classes:

> In the top stream, I think there's just one difficult student there and he has left now. The middle stream . . . rarely if ever would you have [problems], in the present second years now I'm talking about. And the [lower stream] class I'm in charge of you could have up to three suspensions in a week. (Dawes Point, bs wc).

Although formal disciplinary structures were in place in the case-study schools, some personnel expressed dissatisfaction concerning the application of the discipline policy, highlighting inconsistency in dealing with students:

> We're not making a great end of it at the moment; we have problems dealing with discipline . . . he's missing for 2 classes and there's holy war and another fella is missing for 3 weeks and there's nothing done about it, something needs to be done there about it. (Park St. School, bs mxc).

2.5 THE IDENTITY OF SECOND YEARS

Almost all of the key personnel across the schools reported significant differences between first and second year students in their level of confidence and their tendency to misbehave. The exception to this pattern occurred in Dixon St. school, a school with relatively high levels of misbehaviour in first year, where some of the staff reported that students in second year were 'about the same' as they had been in first year. In the remaining schools, students in second year were seen as generally more self-confident which often meant that the second year group were more difficult and disruptive in terms of behaviour:

> They would have been much quieter last year. They are a lot more confident this year . . . they're much more savvy now and much more aware of the things that they can do and get away with you know . . . they've certainly grown in confidence. (Argyle St. School, cd mxc).

> In first year they are quieter, they tend to get a bit cheekier in second year. (Argyle St. School, cd mxc).

> To me they seem the biggest handful . . . when they get to second year they realise that they kind of have the run of the place because they're no longer the children. . . . A lot of changes in personality, people who studied a lot in first year and kind of relaxing then in second year, people who would have been very good, never back answered or give cheek or anything like that, suddenly out of character, snap back or something like that. (Dawson St. School, cd mxc).

> In second year they're coming out of themselves so you've got to be much more disciplinarian with them, that's when they'll test the whole system in second year . . . Second year is a tough year to be a tutor because . . . they're just coming out of their shell. (Dawson St. School, cd mxc).

> They're a little bit cockier, but in second year I think some of the other things then start cropping up, when they get this little bit of confidence, sometimes they can become over confident and it comes out then as maybe behavioural problems or something like that. (Fig Lane School, cd mc).

There was a general feeling among staff that, if students were to misbehave at all, they would be most likely to do so in second year:

They can become a little bit boisterous and if any bullying is to take place it will happen in Second Year . . . as a group they're more problematic in Second Year. (Wattle St. School, bs mxc).

We generally think that second years are more difficult. If they are going to be in trouble second year will be the year. They are more confident. (Argyle St. School, cd mxc).

They tend to come into their own, if they're going to be bold they're going to be bold in second year in class. . . . They've no fear any more. (Barrack St. School, gs wc).

In about half of the interviews, key personnel attributed these changes in behaviour in second year to students' phase of adolescence:

Primarily I think it is biology, it is hormonal, it is . . . wanting to be grown up but not being able to be. (Argyle St. School, cd mxc).

I think it's adolescence, . . . when they get to third year they kind of grow out of it, I think second year is the biggest handful I think as the group I have anyway. (Dawson St. School, cd mxc).

I think it's just the natural part of growing up. (Dawson St. School, cd mxc).

Thing about it is adolescence kicks in and the hormones and so on. (Park St. School, bs mxc).

The growth thing, the hormonal thing, the physical growth and other maturities and guys, their adolescence creeping up on them in second year and that testosterone comes out. (Hay St. School, cd wc).

In other cases, key personnel felt that second year was a difficult year because there is no focus on exams and it can therefore be hard to motivate students:

They're aimless in some ways because there's no focus at the end of second year. The summer exam doesn't carry the weight at all of a state exam . . . Behaviour wise and work wise they're just not as focused, they're aimless in second year. (Argyle St. School, cd mxc).

Then they don't have a state exam at the end of the year so it's still a long time off in third year, the second year is a testing year for a tutor and for the year head, it would be a tough year . . . you see they don't have the state exam. (Dawson St. School, cd mxc).

> I think some of them just think it's a free year to be honest, you just
> try to keep them motivated saying that the exam is coming up but I
> still think they think that's next year, won't worry about it 'til next
> year. (Fig Lane School, cd mc).

> Because there is no big exam at the end of it only the house exam,
> you can find them lacking in motivation from about November. But
> in the middle of second year the motivation goes down. You have to
> be very careful. (Belmore St. School, gs mxc).

Some key personnel mentioned that second year was a crucial year in
shaping the future trajectories of students, with some students becoming
more disengaged in school, and others studying harder and becoming
more engaged as learners:

> I think second year is a very important year. It's a year that they can
> go off the rails or go on the right road to follow on. (Argyle St.
> School, cd mxc).

> It's a crucial year in that they can go one way or the other and it's
> important to keep on top of them and keep them guided and keep
> them directed and focused. (Lang St. School, bs wc).

Some teachers suggested that academically more able students were better able to cope than weaker students:

> Maybe the academically more able guys are able to deal with it in a
> way that the weaker guys can't. (Dawes Point School, bs wc).

> A good class will stay calm and cool but a weaker lad will find him-
> self being challenged far more than he would have been in first year
> and he will tend to react to that. I think definitely the academic work
> becomes more challenging . . ., consequently they act out as a result
> of that and they act out by not producing homework, misbehaving in
> class. (Lang St. School, bs wc).

In sum, all of the school personnel, with the exception of those in Dixon
Street, argue that second year students have a distinct identity, being
generally seen as the most difficult year group at junior cycle level. Students were seen as displaying challenging or difficult behaviour, behaviour which was attributed to their stage of adolescent development as
well as to the lack of an exam focus in second year.

2.6 SUMMARY AND CONCLUSIONS

All of the case-study school provided some support structures for their students in second year but the nature of these structures varied significantly between schools. In all of the case-study schools, the Class Tutor/ Year Head approach formed the core of support for students. However, schools varied in the roles played by Tutors and Year Heads and in the extent to which they were integrated into a school-wide structure. Furthermore, some schools supplemented this approach with support from guidance counsellors or chaplains, and in a few cases, from a matron, student mentors or a home school liaison co-ordinator.

Many of the staff were generally satisfied with the supports they could offer their second year students. Nevertheless, key personnel in all schools felt that there were ways in which supports for students in the school could be improved. The single biggest issue raised was the lack of psychological support for students and key personnel also called for more guidance services for their students. Schools also felt that home-school liaison was of great benefit and should be utilised more to create stronger links between parents and the school.

Closely associated with difficulties in supporting second year students was the issue of bullying. Some schools described second year as a prominent year for bullying issues to arise. Although many of the schools had an anti-bullying policy in place, bullying was still viewed as problematic in several of the schools. Bullying was generally dealt with as a discipline issue within the case-study schools.

The schools generally had very clear discipline procedures for their students. In addition to a pastoral role, Class Tutors and Year Heads tended to play a significant part in enforcing discipline within the school. A number of teachers felt that it was difficult to deal with discipline issues effectively. Second year in particular was described as a time where students were mostly likely to test boundaries and discipline issues were seen as arising most frequently with this group of students.

Almost all key personnel considered second year students as having a unique identity as a year group, with a greater prevalence of misbehaviour and bullying. This was attributed to the stage of adolescence of the students and the lack of an exam focus in second year. As well as an increase in discipline and bullying issues, second year was seen as representing 'a fork in the road' for many students with some students becoming more engaged in schoolwork and others disengaging from school life and becoming more disruptive. Teachers generally felt that academically more able students were able to cope better with the transition to second year.

Chapter Three

LEARNING STRUCTURES IN THE CASE-STUDY SCHOOLS

The case-study schools differ in their practices regarding ability grouping, the timing of subject choice, and teaching methods. Table 3.1 gives an overview of such practices in the twelve case-study schools. Section one discusses school practices in terms of ability grouping in second year. This is followed by an examination of the approaches to subject choice in the case-study schools. Section three examines staff perspectives on the extent to which second-year students are oriented towards the Junior Certificate examination. The approach to assigning homework and carrying out assessment is discussed in section four. The approach to teaching second years and how this approach varies from teaching other year groups is discussed in section five with perceptions of learning support provision outlined in section six.

3.1 ABILITY GROUPING

The case-study schools were selected to capture variation in ability grouping across post-primary schools. 'Streaming' is used to refer to the use of ability test scores to group students into base classes ranked from higher to lower streams. 'Banding' is a looser form of streaming whereby a school may have two 'higher' classes and two 'lower' classes. The prevalence of ability-based differentiation in post-primary schools has declined since the 1980s (Smyth et al., 2004). However, the extent of streaming varies markedly across different types of schools; designated disadvantaged schools and those catering for a higher proportion of

Table 3.1: School profiles

	School Type	Social Mix	School Size	Timing of Subject Choice	Base Class	Use of Setting
Dawson Street	Community/comp.	Mixed	Medium	Pre-entry	Mixed ability	Setting in Irish, English, Maths
Barrack Street	Girls' secondary	Working-class	Small	Pre-entry	Mixed ability	Setting in Irish and Maths
Dixon Street	Vocational	Working-class	Large	Taster programme	Streamed/banded	Level linked to class
Park Street	Boys' secondary	Mixed	Large	Pre-entry	Streamed/banded	Restricted setting for some classes
Hay Street	Vocational	Working-class	Small	Pre-entry	Streamed/banded	Level linked to class
Fig Lane	Fee-paying coed	Middle-class	Large	Taster programme for all of first year	Mixed ability	Setting in Irish and Maths
Argyle Street	Community/comp.	Mixed	Large	Taster programme for all of first year	Streamed/banded	Setting in Irish, English, Maths
Harris Street	Girls' secondary	Middle-class	Large	Taster programme for all of first year	Mixed ability	Setting in Irish and Maths
Lang Street	Vocational	Working-class	Small	Pre-entry	Streamed/banded	Level linked to class
Dawes Point	Boys' secondary	Working-class	Small	Pre-entry	Streamed/banded	Level linked to class
Belmore Street	Girls' secondary	Mixed	Large	Taster programme for all of first year	Mixed ability	Setting in Irish, English, Maths
Wattle Street	Boys' secondary	Mixed	Small	Pre-entry	Mixed ability	Setting in Irish, English, Maths

students with learning difficulties are more likely to use ability-based differentiation than other types of schools. As a result, male students are more likely to attend streamed schools than their female counterparts; data from the *Moving Up* study indicate that 35 per cent of first year boys attend streamed/banded schools compared with 28 per cent of first year girls. Evidence from the 1990s (see Hannan et al., 1996) also indicates that, within streamed schools, male students are more likely to be allocated to lower stream classes than female students.

Although mixed ability grouping is more common now than in the 1990s, being in a mixed ability base class does not necessarily mean that all students are taught in 'mixed ability' classes. Most such schools use 'setting' with students moving to higher and ordinary classes in particular subjects, most commonly, Maths, Irish and English. This is more flexible than streaming since a student may be in the higher Maths class but the lower English class, depending on their ability/performance in each subject. This contrasts with traditional streaming where students tend to be allocated to 'lower' classes for all of their core subjects.

Six of the case-study schools used ability test scores to assign first year students to their class groups. In one of these schools, a looser form of banding was used with one group of lower ability students put into a separate base class and other classes being mixed ability. There is no clear relationship between streaming and the dispersion of ability scores among in-coming students since some of the case-study schools which stream have a very narrow range of ability scores among their students (Smyth et al., 2004). Students in streamed schools tended to stay in the same base classes on moving into second year, although some movement between classes did take place for a small number of students:

> In first year . . . they're streamed and then basically it's the same for second year and third year except guys, maybe two or three, might be moved up or down, depending on their exam results. (Park St., bs mxc)

> In general we look at them individually, there are cases where students are moved because of academic ability or inability, upwards or downwards, depends on the situation but in the main they stay as they are. (Lang St., bs wc)

In the streamed schools, there tended to be a strong relationship between class allocation and the level at which students took subjects, especially the 'core' subjects of Maths, Irish and English. This pattern is consistent with earlier findings from a national survey of post-primary schools (Hannan et al., 1996). Generally, the higher stream classes would be more likely to take higher level while the lower stream classes were more likely to take ordinary or foundation level:

> The teacher sometimes would pick the level. To a great extent the classes are streamed, the class they are in predetermines the level. (Dixon St. School, cd wc).

> They are streamed and it would be mainly [the top class] group that would be taking the higher level subjects. (Hay St., cd wc)

In Park St. school, 'restricted setting' was in place with some of the middle stream classes allowed to move into separate classes for higher level:

> In some situations, say for English, Irish and Maths you're block timetabled so that if a guy is strong enough to do honours, the majority of [the middle stream] would be pass Irish but there's three or four that are good enough for honours and next year now I'm going to put them into another class just for Irish. (Park St., bs mxc)

Although class allocation strongly influenced the subject level taken, a relatively low proportion of students in some of the predominantly working-class schools took higher level so resource constraints meant that some 'core' subject classes had a mixture of students taking higher and ordinary level:[1]

> Because of the nature of our numbers and the resources, teacher availability, if a Maths class is of 20 there may be an example of we'll say 10 of those may wish to do higher level, unfortunately they will not be separated out into a specific group of 10 for higher level, quite often they will stay within the group of 20 and the difficulty comes then with a teacher who wishes to do both grade levels within one group. . . . We wouldn't have the resources to have homogenous honours groups. (Lang St., bs wc).

---

[1] It should be noted, however, that in most cases optional subjects were taught in mixed ability groups.

All of the mixed ability schools maintain mixed ability base classes in second year. However, for some subjects setting is used whereby students are in separate classes for higher and ordinary levels. Setting is used for Irish, English and Maths in Dawson St., Argyle St.[2], Belmore St. and Wattle St. and for Irish and Maths in Barrack St., Harris St. and Fig Lane (see Table 3.1). In most of these schools, performance in first year exams played a strong role in determining whether students were allocated to higher or ordinary level classes:

> The ability grouping in second year is the same as first year except for Irish, English and Maths, where they are based on their scores in those subjects at summer. They may be regrouped into higher and ordinary depending. It's not rigid streaming . . ., it still allows some flexibility in movement. (Argyle St., cd mxc)

> Say for example Maths or English, if they're in possibly an honours class for first year but then they perform quite badly in their summer test and they find they're really, really struggling and they didn't feel that they were going to be able to move on in second year, well then they may drop down to an ordinary level class. (Dawson St., cd mxc)

> I think what they do is they are all left mixed ability up until . . . Halloween in first year. And then there is some streaming done to take out the very bright ones and the very weak ones and then the middle bunch are just left. And then after their exams at . . . February and summer they are re-streamed again, based on results. . . . By the time you get to the end of second year, it's quite strict. (Harris St., gs mc)

However, schools varied in the extent to which students and their parents had an input into the final decision regarding the level they would take. In Wattle St., subject level was quite strongly determined by performance in the first year exams:

> The teachers actually work out that [the levels] for them, it is the top thirty in English, Irish and Maths, so the element of choice is really not there. (Wattle St., bs mxc)

---

[2] In Argyle St., setting is used for students in the 'mixed ability' classes but not for those in the separate lower ability class.

However, in three of the other schools (Dawson St., Harris St. and Fig Lane), recommendations made on the basis of exam results were seen as open to negotiation between teachers, students and their parents:

> Interviewer: And who decides whether the student takes ordinary or higher level?

> It would be a joint sort of thing, the teacher who teaches them on the basis of exam results would recommend and then the parent would come in, you'd have to say that the student and the parent would have the right to say, I would always give them the option if they want to do higher well let them stay with it but . . . I'd make a recommendation and then it's up to the parents, really they have the final decision, I would recommend and then maybe regroup on the basis of that. (Dawson St., cd mxc)

> Well we would generally work it from at the end of first year having a common exam and then try and work classes. Now if there's somebody who would have a particular feeling that their son or daughter has to be in a higher level class, we would co-operate and we'd accommodate that and likewise if somebody felt that I'm quite happy that they do the ordinary level. (Fig Lane, cd mc)

Only staff in Belmore Street school explicitly stated that the ultimate decision is made by the student, albeit with advice given by the subject teacher:

> It is decided this summer now. The teachers of those subjects would give a page around in those classes, and before the summer tests and getting each one to write down what she wishes to do. And does she wish to do higher or ordinary next year. . . . So for the majority their own opinion is right and they are banded themselves. But you would have say out of a 100 you have about maybe 10, where the teacher would have to get talking to the parent. And sometimes the teacher would say ok if you want her to do honours let her do honours, but I do not think she should or vice versa you know. And we would let it go for a year and see how she does. (Belmore St. School, gs mxc).

As well as having advantages in teaching terms, key personnel in Belmore St. school saw setting as facilitating greater social mixing among second year students:

So they [students] meet nearly all the rest of the second years in second year. Whereas they would have had very little cause to meet all
of the first years in first year except for concerts and mass. So they
do get to know more people in second year but they are left with
their same base class. (Belmore St., gs mxc)

In sum, variation in the use of ability grouping is evident across the case-
study schools with distinct consequences for the subject levels taken by
second year students. In the streamed schools, the class to which students
are allocated is a strong influence on the level at which students take subjects. In the mixed ability schools, students remain in mixed base classes
but are in 'set' groups for Maths, Irish and, in most cases, English. Even
where setting is practiced, there is considerable variation in the amount of
input students have into the decision regarding subject levels and the
flexibility of movement between levels. The levels at which students take
their Junior Certificate subjects have longer term consequences for their
Leaving Certificate subjects. Millar and Kelly (1999) found that the level
taken at junior cycle was strongly determinate of the level taken within
senior cycle with only a small proportion of students moving 'upwards'
from ordinary to higher level, especially in Maths. As a result, certain
students in the case-study schools, especially those in lower stream
classes, were very unlikely to be able to access higher level subjects, especially in the 'core' subjects, at senior cycle level.

3.2 SUBJECT CHOICE

The case-study schools varied in the timing of subject choice. In half of
the schools (Wattle Street, Dawson Street, Barrack Street, Park Street,
Hay Street, and Dawes Point), students were required to select their subjects before entering first year. In the other schools (Argyle Street, Harris
Street, Dixon Street, Fig Lane, Lang Street and Belmore Street), students
had a taster programme for part or all of first year where they got to try
out the subjects and then choose which they would like to continue with
for the rest of the junior cycle. These differing approaches had consequences for the number of subjects to which students were exposed.
In first year, the taster programmes meant that some students had an opportunity to try out a wide range of subjects. By second year, some

differences remained between schools in the subjects taken by students. Students across the case-study schools typically took twelve subjects in second year but students in Dawson St., Lang St. and Harris St., schools which were quite different from each other in their socio-economic profile, tended to study thirteen subjects. Students in lower stream classes tended to take fewer subjects on average than those in higher stream classes and, even within mixed ability schools, some students with learning difficulties studied fewer subjects, an issue which is discussed in greater detail in Chapter Five.

The *Moving Up* study (Smyth et al., 2004) indicated that the timing of subject choice meant that students relied on different sources of information in making their decisions. In schools where they had to select subjects before coming to the school, they tended to be more reliant on informal sources of advice, such as parents, siblings and friends, in deciding between subjects. In contrast, students who had the chance to try out subjects before selecting them were in a position to make a more informed choice on the basis of their interests and abilities. Furthermore, students in these schools were more likely to have received information from school personnel on the different subject options.

The issue of subject choice for schools with a taster programme was also raised with key personnel dealing with second year students. Most of these schools said that their students attended an information evening on the subject options along with their parents. Year Heads, subject teachers and Guidance Counsellors were all mentioned as involved in giving students advice on subject choice. Two of the schools, Fig Lane and Argyle St., appeared to have a stronger input from guidance counsellors into the choice process:

Interviewer: How do they [students] know what to choose?

They know because they have had the subjects in first year. There has been a parent meeting on the issue, a night meeting. The guidance team are available to the first years in the spring of their first year. Then there is a recheck in September by the guidance team that everybody is happy and there is a re-opt if space allows at the end of September. (Argyle St. School, cd mxc).

In one school there was concern about the lack of choice available to lower stream classes and the fact that they were not allowed to take some of the more practically orientated subjects:

> The subjects don't change [between first and second year] but they don't have access to Art or Home Economics, which I think is a pity. I would have a lot in my class now who would very much thrive on using their hands and practical subjects. And I think even creativeness, I have a lot of creative students that don't get that, except maybe in religion or other subjects like CSPE, but they wouldn't get the chance to use that creativity. (Dixon St. School, cd wc).

Another concern was that, in spite of the benefits of having a taster programme, it also had the disadvantage of taking time away from covering the junior cycle course:

> From my perspective it [the taster programme] works out very badly . . . What happens is we then end up in second year when they take [my subject] trying to do the three-year Junior Cert course in the two years. So the cons are that we lose a huge amount of time but the benefits then are that those who choose [my subject] in second year want to do it. (Harris St. School, gs mc).

In sum, variation between the case-study schools in their approach to subject choice meant that students relied on different sources of information and advice in making their selection. Over and above the impact of the choice process, schools differed to some extent in the number of subjects taken by their students.

3.3 ORIENTATION TOWARDS THE JUNIOR CERTIFICATE EXAMINATION

Key personnel in the case-study schools were asked about the extent to which second year students were oriented towards the Junior Certificate examination. The vast majority of key personnel felt that the second year students were generally not thinking about the Junior Certificate except for possibly a few focussed students, responses which were consistent with the lack of an exam focus in second year discussed in Chapter Two:

> Well I think some of them would be pretty focused you know . . . some of them would be very focused. (Argyle Street, cd mxc).

Interviewer: And do you think they're thinking about the Junior Cert at this stage?

The second years? No. I don't think they ever tend to think about it, no. (Barrack Street, gs wc).

Interviewer: Do you think in second year they think about exams?

Not for a minute [laughing], not for a minute. They prefer not to. (Dixon Street, cd wc).

In four of the streamed schools, key personnel distinguished among the class groups, reporting that students in the higher stream classes were more likely to be thinking about the Junior Certificate at this stage:

I think only the really top stream would be thinking of any examinations. (Dixon Street, cd wc).

They'd be quite focused now, the [top stream] would be quite focused, the others mightn't be thinking too much about it or taking it too seriously, they would be doing the pass of course, the other class. (Park Street, bs mxc).

I'd say the weaker students hardly [think about it] at all because it's something they want to kind of dismiss into the distance. In some cases I would say a very small minority of students, a very small minority would . . . have an awareness you're doing an exam in third year. (Dawes Point, bs wc).

Some key personnel also feel that it is the students' background that influences whether the student is thinking about the Junior Certificate:

Interviewer: And to what extent do you think they are thinking about the Junior Cert at this stage?

It varies from family to family and child to child. The children [who] come from very well motivated families and the parents are educated and they are very pushy for them. Those children will keep very well motivated . . . and the area that they come from and the family that they come from. We would have some parts of the town where if children come from that area it is very hard to motivate them. And attendance can be low enough. (Belmore Street, gs mxc).

One staff member in a working-class school suggested that, if there was continuous assessment, students would be more aware of the Junior Certificate instead of viewing it as an exam in the distant future:

> The type of kids we have, it's just live for the day too. And it's very hard to get them to sort of think ahead and plan ... but say . . . if they had a different curriculum or if it's project based and continuous assessment you know, that would bring it home much more. But if it's an external exam in year three . . ., they don't start thinking about it you know. (Barrack Street, gs wc).

While staff reported that many students were not thinking about the Junior Certificate, this did not mean that key personnel were not trying to make the students aware of the exam. Many of the key personnel said that they had been talking about the exam to their students:

> They are not thinking about it but we are certainly talking about it. And they tend [then] to start thinking about it. (Argyle Street, cd mxc).

> I doubt they're thinking about it at all . . . you know, you keep mentioning Junior Cert. to them but it's beyond them really. (Harris Street, gs mc).

> Interviewer: So do they start thinking of the Junior Cert exams at this stage in their second year?

> The teachers do anyway, whatever about the students. Presumably probably the better ones do but it's not very, very obvious. (Wattle Street, bs mxc).

Although many of the key personnel agreed that students are not yet thinking of the Junior Certificate, this was not normally seen as a negative issue, and some indicated that they felt it was too early for second year students to be thinking about the Junior Certificate:

> I don't think that it really impacts that much, . . . I think a year away is miles in their lives and that's the way I like it to be, do you know. I don't think it's necessary to have that hanging over them, while I think it's very good in third year. (Harris Street, gs mc).

> I suppose at that stage teachers and students think about just doing the said work rather than actually focussing on an exam. And I think I'm happier with that as well . . . there's enough of focus on the

exam without, you know, reminding them too early about it. (Wattle Street, cd mxc).

3.4 HOMEWORK AND ASSESSMENT

Approaches to teaching and assessment are discussed in this and the following section. These accounts are based on the key personnel who were involved in teaching second year students. While their perceptions cannot be taken of wholly representative of all teachers taking second year students in the case-study schools, they do yield useful insights into variation across the schools analysed.

3.4.1 Homework

Most key personnel reported giving their students some homework but the approaches to homework varied between schools and within some schools. Discussions of homework were not generally framed in terms of a set homework policy within the school. Three schools said they did not have such a policy, two said they were in the process of drafting a policy while two schools said they had a homework policy in place. There were, however, certain expectations about the amount of time that students would spend on homework and study with a number of staff citing two hours as a target:

> Well in our journal we suggest a certain amount of time, we would be talking about two hours and that would be divided between homework and study and we would expect them then to put in two hours over the weekend on study as well but there would be quite a number of them who wouldn't be doing that at all. (Dawson St. School, cd mxc).

> We talk about two to two and a half hours [homework] in the evening. We would be quite happy actually if it just hit the two . . . That time is made available by the school [through supervised study], the option is there for them and we think that realistically that would be okay. (Wattle St. School, bs mxc).

The actual amount of time students themselves report spending on homework and study will be discussed in Chapter Five below.

Generally, variation was evident within schools in the amount of homework given. In some of the streamed schools, teachers appeared to vary the amount of homework given depending on the ability level of the class group. Generally, key personnel described giving the top stream more homework than the lower stream class:

> Oh yeah [I give them homework], every single night. . . . the weak fellas I don't . . . I don't give them homework at all . . . I think in a lot of subjects a lot of teachers have the same approach because they won't do it and you're kind of fighting with them then and you know . . . you can actually get away with doing most of the work in class and even keeping the books in class and stuff like that. Because they lose things and . . . they just can't organise themselves you know.

> Interviewer: Whereas with the top stream you'd tend to give them homework?

> Oh you'd load them with work. (Dawes Point, bs wc)

This pattern is consistent with findings from British research which indicates that students in lower stream classes tend to be assigned less homework than those in the higher streams (Hallam and Ireson, 2005).

3.4.2 Assessment

Almost all of the key personnel gave class tests as well as having formal tests in the school throughout the year. These class tests were normally given at the end of a chapter or section of work:

> On completion of chapters, then mid terms, Christmas, summer. (Dawson Street, cd mxc).

> At the end of every chapter we have a test. (Harris Street, gs mc).

> I would give fairly regular tests, usually at the end of whatever section it is that we're doing, they would get a test. (Park Street, bs mxc).

The main reasons that key personnel gave for assessing students were to monitor the student's progress and to give them feedback on how they were progressing:

To see how well they understand what I've taught in class and how much of it they have learned and to see how hard they're working and to see how well they're progressing or if they're disimproving. (Fig Lane, cd mc).

Just to check that they are actually progressing. (Lang Street, bs wc).

They can then sort of gauge themselves if they so wish against the whole year rather than just being their class . . . that they can sort of gauge their position rather than just in their own class. (Fig Lane, cd mc).

Teachers were less likely to mention monitoring their own practice as a central goal of assessment, although teachers in Arygle St. school were more likely to take this approach:

Interviewer: Why do you use tests at all? What do you try to find out?

I suppose a couple of things, from my own point of view just for me to try and do things better. If I find that everybody has got something that I have been plugging away at over and over again and they still haven't got it right, obviously there is something wrong with me. (Argyle St., cd mxc)

I think a teacher has to assess as they go through the term. Because otherwise you can find yourself giving the big test at Christmas or summer and finding that your students don't understand what you were saying. (Argyle St., cd mxc).

3.5 TEACHING SECOND YEAR STUDENTS

An analysis of teaching practices used with first year students indicated a relatively strong reliance on more traditional didactic methods (Smyth et al., 2004). When asked about teaching second year students, the most common response was to report that the teachers tried to relate the subject or topic to the student and to engage the student in the topic:

Well it would be getting them involved and trying to relate it to their own experiences . . . bring in real life into the class and trying to relate it to what they know. (Belmore Street, gs mxc).

You must maintain their interest . . . active learning is very, very important. (Dawes Point School, cd mxc).

> Try and relate it to what they are doing at home. (Argyle Street, cd mxc).

The teachers saw activity-based learning and practical work as important techniques for engaging the students. However, second year students were somewhat less likely to report these approaches as characteristic of their day to day classes (see Chapter Five). Staff in some schools, such as Fig Lane School and Dawson Street (both mixed ability, mixed/middle-class schools), spoke more about using practical activities than others:

> They'd always have practical work every week. (Fig Lane School, cd mc).

> Learning by doing . . . So it would be quite sort of practical based. (Fig Lane School, cd mc).

> I try as far as possible to make it experiential learning. (Dawson Street, cd mxc).

> I do try to make it a bit fun if I can . . . so I like to do some experiments every week if I can. (Dawson Street, cd mxc).

Furthermore, a number of teachers reported pair-work or allowing students to work in small groups within their classes:

> Sometimes they can work in groups and come back [and] give me feedback. (Argyle Street, cd mxc).

> Sometimes it would be group work . . . if they're working in class they may work in groups, groups of two generally. (Dawson Street, cd mxc).

> Some days I would use group work, other days I would use pair work . . . usually they love pair work and they work really well under that. (Dawson Street, cd mxc).

> They'd work in groups . . . they'd work in groups themselves for maybe project based work as well. (Fig Lane School, cd mc).

However, only one teacher reported grouping students in such a way as to maximise exchange between students and learning within the group:

> Let them work in groups of two and three. They can feed off each other . . . generally I try to divide them up in the groups . . . a strong

> student, middle-range student and a weak student, so that, you know, hopefully it all filters around. (Wattle Street, bs mxc).

Staff in three schools, Argyle Street, Dawson Street and Fig Lane, were more likely than those in other schools to report using a range of different teaching techniques. All three schools were mixed ability and mixed/middle-class in their student intake. This pattern is consistent with previous research which indicates that students in more disadvantaged school contexts may be exposed to less challenging pedagogical and curricular experiences (see Conway, 2002).

A small group of teachers felt they had to adapt their teaching methods considerably with the less academically able students. This was often conveyed in a seemingly negative light, comparing the weak classes to better classes who were seen as 'easier' to teach. The following quotes are representative of these views:

> With the first year group that I have I mean they are just like . . . an ideal class, if you tell them things once and they get it and you can move on from topic to topic. With the second year I have [the set] group . . . you have to explain things really, like really back to basics . . . the foundation class I have they are very weak, I mean they are weak across the board, in all of their subjects. (Harris Street, gs mc).

> You know with these fellas like you know they're so weak that you kind of have to abandon the book you know . . . Like I have another second year group but they're kind of brighter . . . they'd be good second years now, very good second years. Like . . . there's no problem with them like dealing with them you know. (Dawes Point, bs wc).

> It would have to be as simplified as possible and I find that this group because they are terribly weak, maybe writing on the backboard does not work very well in that they can't concentrate that far away from them, that might sound extreme but they can't. (Lang Street, bs wc).

The use of different teaching methods with different ability groups echoes British research (Hallam and Ireson, 2005) which found that lower stream classes tend to have greater emphasis on repetition, more structured work and a slower pace of instruction than higher stream classes.

Teachers reported using different approaches in teaching second years than in teaching first year students; one of the main differences mentioned was that teachers were less strict with first year students but expected students to be settled in by second year:

> You'd probably be more conscious of the fact that some fellas are finding it difficult to settle in we'll say in first year, whereas when you have a guy in second year he's more experienced, he's more street wise as regards the school so you wouldn't be generally as sympathetic to him . . . For example a fella who wouldn't have his homework done in first year and you can sense maybe that there's something more . . ., then I'd just leave him and say well try and do it tonight if you can, that kind of thing, whereas in second year you might deal with it a bit differently, lay down the law and say that's not good enough and you might give them some sort of a punishment for not doing it. (Park Street, bs mxc).

> I think a lot of the time the first years you treat them a lot of the time with kid gloves that you're very mammy towards them . . . whereas in second year it levels out. (Fig Lane, cd mc).

> Well in first year you would have to go softly, softly. Because . . . they are in a big school now and it can be difficult for some of them to deal with a big school . . . But second years should be settled and sorted themselves out and chosen subjects that they want to do and be happy enough with those subjects . . . so they should have settled down. (Belmore Street, gs mxc).

3.6 LEARNING SUPPORT

The *Moving Up* study (Smyth et al., 2004) indicated variation across schools in the availability of learning support, that is, in additional assistance given to students with learning difficulties, as well as in the perceived adequacy of such support. The profile of students receiving learning support in second year will be discussed in Chapter Five. The issue of learning support provision for second year students was discussed with principals in the case-study schools, although it was raised as an issue by some of the other key personnel. Three of the schools (Fig Lane, Dixon St. and Wattle St.) were broadly satisfied with existing provision:

> The learning support in this school is quite well developed in that we have about six people who are fully trained and then we have a year

head, or an assistant principal in charge of the area and who administers the learning support . . . the college of education actually send people out to see how we are doing, they think we are doing it okay. (Dixon Street, cd wc).

Well we do have remedial teachers here that take them on a one to one, literally every day and they take them for the subjects that they're weak in and then we have an opportunity, we're only after getting a notice if you have other students you think should partake in that kind of care, just to identify them and their subjects that they're weak in and we cater for it, so it's quite good. (Fig Lane, cd mc).

I am absolutely delighted with it [learning support provision] and long may it continue. (Wattle Street, bs mxc).

Staff in the remainder of the case-study schools expressed dissatisfaction with the amount of learning support they were able to offer their students. The biggest concern amongst the schools was the issue of resources:

I feel it's inadequate. Like for example, like we have one full-time learning support teacher okay, and we don't have any resource teacher . . . we put in an application last year for nearly fifty kids in the school who've got learning difficulties and we got like ten extra hours for all, for those kids on top of the learning support . . . there are kids in the school getting no support because we just don't have the hours to give them. (Harris Street, gs mc).

We would get hours allocated to us for special cases but we will never get what we request. I might request 15 resource hours for the week and I might get two and a half, that's the reality of it unfortunately, then we divvy those up among the teachers who are available for resource work. (Lang Street, bs wc).

Another school reported that their provision levels had been cut back in recent years:

I was [satisfied]. Our school did well because our psychologists were pleased with the way that we used our hours and the way we combined and made sure every single minute was used . . . but since the money fell through I found now they were much sharper. We lost two that we got before this year on a technical point. And I feel this year coming again any little technical point . . . we would not get it unless it is written down very clearly and the nature of the help and the time of it by the psychologist. And I fear for that now and the same for the traveller support, you know, and for non-national support. (Belmore Street, gs mxc).

The issue of inadequate language support for 'new-comer' students was also raised in Barrack Street, which had experienced a reduction in provision:

A lot of those [recently immigrated students] have learning difficulties around English. Now last year . . . we had two TEFL [Teaching English as a Foreign Language] teachers . . . they withdrew the two TEFL teachers last summer. So we have . . . no intensive teaching of English for foreign students, you know, . . . and we've twenty percent of our kids are foreign students. (Barrack Street, gs wc).

3.7 CONCLUSIONS

The case-study schools adopted the same approach to grouping students into base classes in second year as they had in first year. However, among the mixed ability schools, ability-based differentiation was put in place for Maths, Irish and, for the most part, English. These schools varied, however, in the amount of choice given to students regarding the subject level they pursued along with the degree of flexibility allowed in relation to movement between levels. Within the streamed schools, the class to which students were allocated was strongly predictive of the exam level they would take and thus ability grouping at junior cycle can have longer term consequences regarding access to subject levels for the Leaving Certificate. Although students were already allocated to different levels for many subjects in second year, key personnel tended to feel that second years were not yet thinking very much about the Junior Certificate examination. An exception related to some of the higher stream classes who were seen as more strongly oriented towards the exam.

The case-study schools varied in the timing of subject choice with implications for the kind of information and advice students drew on in making their decisions. Schools also influenced the curricular experiences of their students by deciding how many subjects they would take; students in lower stream classes and/or those with learning difficulties tended to take a more restricted set of subjects. Some differences were evident between schools in the approach to teaching and assessment. Teachers generally used assessment in the form of class tests to monitor students' progress and were less likely to mention that the results influenced their approach to teaching the class group. Some variation in teaching styles was apparent within schools in terms of the ability level of students with a greater emphasis on the 'basics' with lower stream classes. As in first year, the majority of the case-study schools were dissatisfied with the learning support provision they could put in place for students.

Chapter Four

THE SOCIAL CLIMATE OF THE SCHOOL AND CLASSROOM — STUDENT PERSPECTIVES

Chapters Two and Three have explored school support and learning structures from the point of view of key personnel dealing with second year
students. This chapter looks at the social climate of the school and classroom from students' own perspectives. It draws on questionnaires completed by 905 students in the twelve case-study schools along with group
interviews conducted with second year students. The chapter describes
experiences among different groups of students in terms of their gender,
social background, reading and maths scores in first year[1], and their academic self-rating, that is, how they compare their academic performance
to that of other students in their class or year group. It also relates these
experiences to the context at the class, especially ability group, and the
school level, focusing in particular on the existence of formalised support
structures and on the social mix of students in the school.

The first three sections discuss informal social relations within the
school, that is, the nature and quality of interaction between teachers and
students and among students themselves. The fourth section analyses
students' views on the disciplinary climate in the school, focusing in particular on self-reported incidence of misbehaviour and school strategies
for dealing with such behaviour. Section five looks at the extent to which
students are engaged in school life while section six examines student
self-image across a range of dimensions, including perceived academic
ability and body-image.

---

[1] These ability test data are available only for the ten schools who participated in year
one of the study.

4.1 TEACHER-STUDENT RELATIONS IN THE SCHOOL

4.1.1 Positive teacher-student interaction

The survey of students collected information on the frequency of positive and negative interaction between teachers and students in the school. The measure of positive teacher-student interaction was based on the extent to which students had been told their work was good by a teacher, had asked questions in class, had been asked questions in class, had been praised for asking a question, and had been praised for doing their written work well. The majority of students (61%) had been asked questions in class often or very often while over half had themselves asked questions in class frequently (see Figure 4.1). Praise from teachers was less frequent with 41 per cent being told their work was good often or very often, 30 per cent were praised for an answer in class and 34 per cent were praised for their written work. Although positive interaction between teachers and students was fairly prevalent across the case-study schools, a significant proportion of students (25%) reported never having been praised for their answers or written work.

These different aspects of student-teacher interaction were used to form a composite measure of positive student-teacher interaction.[2] The components of this measure along with the other scales used in the chapter are outlined in the appendix. There were no significant differences by gender in the level of positive interaction with teachers. Positive interaction is somewhat more commonly reported by students newly arrived in Ireland, though the difference from other students is not marked. The relationship with students' own ability levels is complex; students who had lower reading and maths scores in first year tend to report more positive interaction with their teachers, perhaps reflecting greater teacher encouragement for this group of students. However, in terms of students' academic self-rating, those who deemed themselves 'above average' reported the highest level of positive interaction; it would appear, there-

---

[2] The resulting scale had a reliability of 0.77, using Cronbach's alpha. This measure assesses the extent to which a set of items are interrelated, that is, can be treated as measuring a single latent variable. As a rule of thumb, a value of 0.7 or higher is taken as indicating high reliability.

fore, that teacher encouragement plays some role in boosting students' perceptions of their own abilities, an issue that is explored further in Chapter Six.

Figure 4.1: Positive teacher-student interaction

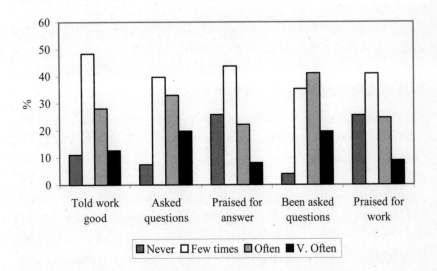

Interestingly, the highest levels of positive interaction are found among students in lower stream classes in streamed/banded schools; this pattern of higher positive interaction among the lower stream than the upper stream applies within streamed/banded schools (with the exception of Dawes Point and Argyle Street). This pattern may reflect the effect of smaller class sizes in lower stream classes and/or a deliberate strategy on the part of teachers to encourage student achievement through positive reinforcement. The prevalence of positive interaction also varies across the case-study schools. On the whole, students in schools serving more working-class populations tend to report more positive interaction; thus, the highest levels of positive teacher-student interaction were reported in Barrack St., Dixon St. and Lang St. schools, all designated disadvantaged schools. However, there is some variation within this group of schools since Dawes Point school, also a designated disadvantaged school, has among the lowest levels of positive interaction. There is no simple relationship between levels of positive teacher-student interaction and the existence of formal support structures for second years in the school. Two of the three schools with the highest levels of positive interaction were found to have relatively weak support structures for second years while two of the three schools with low levels of positive interaction have relatively strongly developed structures in place. It would appear, therefore, that the existence of formalised structures is not sufficient to guarantee a positive classroom climate unless relations between staff and students are positive at an informal level.

4.1.2 Negative teacher-student interaction

Negative teacher-student interaction was measured in terms of the frequency with which students reported having been 'given out to' by teachers. Over a quarter of the students surveyed had been frequently given out to for misbehaving in class while over a fifth had been frequently given out to because of their schoolwork not being done on time or properly (see Figure 4.2). A significant minority of students had not been given out to by teachers at all in the two weeks prior to the survey. Interestingly, there is no significant relationship between levels of positive and negative interaction with teachers. It would appear that some students may attract both positive and negative attention while others may avoid the attention of teachers to a significant extent.

The pattern of negative interaction[3] varied significantly by gender with male students reporting being given out to more frequently than their female counterparts. This gender difference is also evident within coed schools, indicating that males experience more negative interaction with their teachers than females in the same school context. The level of negative interaction also varied by social class with students from professional or farming backgrounds experiencing less negative interaction with their teachers than students from other social backgrounds; in contrast, students from Travelling backgrounds are more likely to report negative interaction with teachers. Negative interaction varies significantly by academic ability/performance; students with lower reading and maths scores and those who rate themselves as below average are more likely to report being given out to by teachers.

---

[3] The composite measure of negative student-teacher interaction has a reliability of 0.74.

Figure 4.2: Negative teacher-student interaction

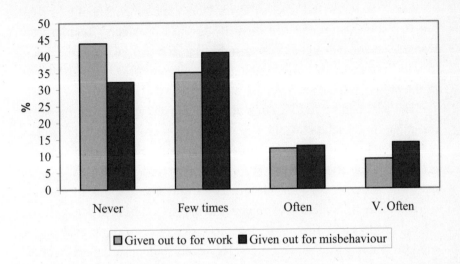

Students in lower stream classes in streamed schools tend to report the highest levels of negative interaction with the lowest levels found in mixed ability classes; the exceptions to the pattern of higher negative interaction among the lower stream than among the higher stream are found within Lang St. and Dixon St. schools. Thus, students in lower stream classes tend to experience higher levels of both positive and negative teacher-student interaction, most likely reflecting smaller class sizes among these groups of students.

The prevalence of negative interaction tends to be greater in schools with a concentration of working-class students, a pattern which is at least in part related to the greater use of streaming in these schools; thus, the highest levels of negative interaction are found in Lang St. and Dixon St. schools, both designated disadvantaged schools and schools with high average levels of positive interaction. However, the lowest levels of negative interaction are found in two of the girls' schools, Belmore St. and Barrack St., the latter a designated disadvantaged school. As with positive teacher-student relations, there is no simple relationship between levels of negative teacher-student interaction and the existence of formal support structures for second years in the school, though there is some evidence that the lowest level of negative interaction is found in mixed/middle-class schools with formalised structures.

4.1.3 Willingness of students to approach teachers

Chapter Two discussed whether Class Tutors and other school personnel felt that students approached them if they had problems. Relations between teachers and students can also be assessed by looking at the extent to which students themselves felt they could approach teachers with a problem.

The vast majority (85%) of students surveyed agreed with the statement that 'my teachers would help me if I had a problem with my school work'. Female students were more likely than boys to agree with the statement. Traveller students were somewhat more likely to disagree with this statement but the differences from other groups of students were not marked. Overall, willingness to approach teachers is not clearly related to the social mix of students in a school or to the prevalence of support structures for second years. However, students are more likely to be willing to go to teachers with academic problems if they have had positive interaction with their teachers and less likely to do so if their interaction has been negative. This highlights the importance of considering the informal climate of the school, that is, the quality of interaction between teachers and students, as well formal policies in looking at the impact on personal-social development among students.

The proportion of students who said that 'I could talk to at least one of my teachers if I had a problem' was lower than the proportion who said they could go with a schoolwork-related problem but still high at two-thirds of students in the case-study schools. There were no significant gender differences in responses to this statement. However, students from minority groups (Traveller and immigrant children) were somewhat more likely to agree with this statement than other student groups, supporting the greater reliance on key personnel among certain 'at risk' students found in first year (see Smyth et al., 2004). Those in lower stream classes were somewhat more likely to see their teachers as approachable than students in other class types, most likely reflecting the greater degree of contact they have with their teachers. Interestingly, the pattern of responses did not vary significantly by school. However, informal relations within the school play a strong role; as might be expected, students who experience high levels of negative interaction with their teachers are less likely to find their teachers approachable while those who experience high levels of positive interaction with teachers are much more likely to be willing to go to their teachers with a problem.

In the group interviews, students were asked whether they would go to a teacher if they had a problem. Generally students said they would not approach a teacher with a problem:

Interviewer: If you had a problem do you think you'd go to any of your teachers?

Student: No.

Student: It depends what the problem is, if it's like a really big problem then, no.

Student: If it's got to do with like your friends or somebody at home, your personal life, you probably wouldn't. (Harris Street, mixed ability class, girls' school, mc).

Some students felt they could, at least in theory, approach their Class Tutor if they had a problem. However, the class groups generally saw the role of the Class Tutor as mainly a disciplinary one and the main contact many classes had with their tutor was for registration. As a result, few classes believed they would go to their Class Tutor if they had a problem:

Interviewer: What does the class tutor do in this school?

Student: Give out to you.

Students: Yeah.

Student: Not really, if you get in trouble with a teacher, the teacher will tell the tutor and he just kind of sorts you out.

Interviewer: So it's mostly for giving out to you, is it?

Students: Yeah.

Student: He doesn't really do anything, the one we have this year is a bit dodgy.

Interviewer: Do you think you could go to them if you had a problem?

Student: No.

Student: No. (Park St. School, boys' school, middle stream class, mxc).

In some schools, the students felt that it would be easier to go to other members of staff, such as the Guidance Counsellor, chaplain or matron in the school. Students often mentioned that they would prefer to talk to either younger teachers or student mentors/buddies:

> Student: I think it's kind of the more younger teachers you'd kind of bring your problems to because you don't feel that kind of connected with the older ones you know. Like the younger ones tend to get to know you a lot better and stuff, like especially like the H.Dips, we'd loads of H.Dips last year and they're really nice now, they got to know you and stuff. They're more friends; well they're kind of more friendly like in a way. But still . . . the other teachers are friendly too but you know the others would be like more friendlier. (Argyle Street, higher band, coed school, mxc).

Some classes also felt that there was an issue of confidentiality when approaching teachers with problems or that teachers could not always help the students with their problems, particularly with what were seen as more serious problems such as bullying:

> Student: Well sometimes you have no choice, like just say you're in school, like in school or say you start crying or something or like at registration and your teacher pulls you up and they're going what's wrong and make you tell them.

> Student: And you don't want to.

> Student: Yeah and they're kind of like mixed in with it and all and you just don't want them to, but they kind of find out anyway.

> Student: Yeah, they get involved by talking to you.

> Student: Yeah.

> Student: Yeah and I think like that's happened before and like they might have got what's wrong out of you but then . . . they wouldn't keep it confidential, well they'd keep it confidential but they try get into it and try to fix it and . . . you wouldn't want them to . . ., they start ringing your parents and saying all the stuff and you wouldn't want them to do any of that.

> Student: Unless you wanted them to, like sometimes you might want them to sort out something that happened in school or at lunchtime even.

Student: They kind of make the problem worse in a way when they get involved. (Harris St. School, girls' school, mixed ability class, mc).

On initial investigation, there appears to be an inconsistency between the survey responses and what the students said when interviewed in a group context. In the survey, the majority of students indicated that they agreed with the statement 'I could talk to at least one of my teachers if I had a problem' and yet, when interviewed, the majority said they would not approach a teacher with a problem. This may be because students felt that while they could go to a teacher in theory, they would be unlikely to actually do so if a problem arose, thus contrasting 'she says you can [go to her]' and 'nobody goes though' (Barrack St girls' school, wc).

There may also be a difference between the two contexts in terms of the kinds of situations in which students would approach a teacher with a problem. Students may have interpreted the questionnaire statement as relating to more general school-related problems; however, in the group interviews, students were specifically prompted about whether they would go to a teacher in relation to a personal problem. The difference in re-sponses between the survey and the group interviews may also relate to students' being unwilling to admit in front of their classmates that they have gone, or would be prepared to go, to a teacher if they had difficulties.

In terms of more general interaction with teachers, the majority of class groups said that they got on with at least some of their teachers. A significant minority felt that they got on with most of their teachers and only three of the class groups said that they didn't get on with their teachers at all. Students felt that their relationship with their teachers of-ten depended on the particular teacher and their personality traits:

Interviewer: How do the students get on with teachers?

Student: All right.

Student: Some teachers are bang on, some teachers are moan bags and no one ever talks to them.

Student: We don't get along with them properly.

Student: They're eejits. (Dixon St. School, coed school, lower stream class, wc).

Student: The teachers like can be kind of sound and then . . . you wish like you had a different teacher but sometimes you get on with them and sometimes you don't like.

Student: It kind of depends on their mood and your mood on the day, like if they're in a bad mood and you mess or something they take their bad mood out on you so . . .

Student: I have to say they get on [with us].

Student: They get on most days anyway so. (Wattle St. School, boys' school, mixed ability class, mxc).

The survey responses indicated that students in lower stream classes tended to have the highest average levels of positive and of negative inter-action with their teachers, reflecting at least in part the smaller class sizes for these groups. Students in these classes tended to characterise their overall relationships with their teachers in negative terms, with a 'them and us' view. It should be noted that some teachers in streamed schools expressed the view that they found teaching the lower stream groups more difficult (see Chapter Three), perhaps contributing to this negative class-room climate. One class group in Park St. boys' school felt that their teachers 'don't care about us' and contrasted that with the treatment of the other classes: 'they [teachers] trust them, they let them do things'. A num-ber of the lower stream classes reported that they tended to be singled out for blame when misbehaviour occurred, although in some cases they ac-knowledged this occurred because of previous discipline incidents:

Student: The teachers are more annoying this year, . . . they're pick-ing on us.

. . .

Student: The teachers blame you for everything.

. . .

Student: There's a good crowd of teachers we don't get along with and they don't get along with us.

Student: Exactly.

Student: It's their fault, they don't get along with us.

. . .

Student: The teachers think they can just shout at you for nothing, there's a teacher there now called Ms. [name] and she thinks she can shout at you for nothing.

Student: You're never going to do good in school.

Student: She'd say you're only wasting, she'd be mocking people.

. . .

Student: They couldn't be bothered with us really. (Lang St. School, boys' school, lower stream, wc).

Student: The bad thing is after [an incident of misbehaviour] everyone just started blaming stuff on us if something happened. . . .

Student: Yeah, if something happened we'd get blamed.

. . .

Student: Keys got robbed and we were blamed for it. (Dawes Point, boys' school, lower stream, wc)

In sum, the nature of relations between teachers and students appeared to vary across the case-study schools and between class groups within schools. The extent to which second years felt that some groups of students were treated unequally by teachers is explored in the following section.

4.2 PERCEPTIONS REGARDING EQUALITY OF TREATMENT

Students were not only asked about their relations with teachers in general but also about the extent to which different groups of students were treated equally within the school. Sixty per cent of students reported that teachers treated the different class groups differently (see Figure 4.3). Teachers were seen as favouring hardworking students (69%) and clever students (51%). However, over one-third of students reported that teachers in their school did not have 'favourites'. Treatment was not generally seen to reflect gender or national background; 29 per cent of students felt that boys and girls were not treated equally in their school while 16 per cent reported that Irish students were treated better than those from overseas.

Figure 4.3: Perceptions in relation to unequal treatment of students

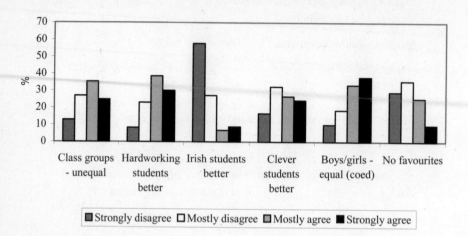

As might be expected, students in streamed schools are more likely to report differential treatment of class groups; perhaps surprisingly, those in the higher stream classes are more likely to report unequal treatment. In addition, those in streamed schools, especially those in lower stream classes, are more likely to report that teachers have favourites:

> If a teacher didn't like someone now and they didn't have their homework done they'd get killed and if someone that he liked didn't have their homework done he'd just say do it the next day, that's unfair. (Lang St. school, boys' school, lower stream, wc)

Students in streamed schools are also more likely to think that teachers favour hard-working students. Those in higher stream classes are most likely to say that teachers favour clever students and those in lower stream classes least likely to do so. Students who rate themselves as below average are more likely to think that teachers have favourites and that they favour hard-working and clever students. The greatest perceived inequality of treatment was reported in Lang St. school, a streamed school with very negative teacher-student relations within the lower streams, and was least prevalent in Belmore St. and Fig Lane schools, both of whom used mixed ability grouping.

The issue of unequal treatment of groups of students was also raised by some students in the group interviews. The questionnaire data indicated that students in the lower streams in streamed schools were most likely to agree that teachers have favourites, a pattern that does not emerge clearly from the group interviews with students. It may be that some students were less likely to discuss the issue where they were in a group with other students who were deemed 'favourites'. Many students felt some teachers were unfair to particular students or had favourite students in the class. This was most prevalent amongst class groups in Harris Street, Fig Lane and Belmore Street, all mixed ability schools, as well as in Argyle Street:

> Some teachers have favourites. (Harris Street, mixed ability class, girls' school, mc).

> Student: They [teachers] pick on you, they don't like you, yourself.

> Student: They've a favourite. (Fig Lane, mixed ability class, coed school, mc).

> Student: They have their favourites in their class and they don't really like anyone else.

> Student: And they ignore you.

> Student: And if they like you they would ask you all the questions and if they do not like you they would completely ignore you. They expect you to know everything if they like you and they expect you to know nothing if they do not like you.

> Student: And some teachers if they hate you they would pick on you. And you are just 'leave me alone'. (Belmore St. School, girls' school, mixed ability class, mxc).

The issue of teachers treating students unequally on the basis of gender arose in a number of interviews with groups of students, particularly in Argyle Street, Fig Lane and Dixon Street, schools with very different student intakes in terms of social background. However, students within Argyle St. and Fig Lane schools disagreed about whether male or female students were favoured and whether teacher gender played a part in this:

> Student: The female teachers and the girls get on a lot more than the lads. (Argyle Street, higher band, coed school, mxc).

Student: Well like male teachers normally get on better with the girls.

Student: They're always laughing with the girls. (Argyle Street, higher band, coed school, mxc).

I think that the male teachers treat us the same as the lads and the women teachers treat me the same, I don't notice anything like that. (Argyle Street, lower band, coed school, mxc).

Student: But favourites are always more likely to be girls, that's what I think anyway, very few lads [are] favourites. (Fig Lane, mixed ability class, coed school, mc).

Students in Dixon Street were the only ones who consistently felt that both male and female teachers treated female students more favourably:

Student: They do nothing to the girls.

Student: We [boys] get the blame for it.

. . .

Student: The girl teachers stick up for the girls and the boys stick up for the girls as well. (Dixon Street, middle stream, coed school, wc).

Although some students reported that girls and boys were not treated equally within coeducational schools, coeducation was seen as a more popular option among students than single-sex schooling. Students were asked about whether they would prefer to be in a single-sex rather than a coed school. In general, the majority of all students, whether male or female and whether in a coed or single-sex school, expressed a preference for coeducational schooling (Figure 4.4). The vast majority of both male and female students in coed schools expressed a preference for attending a coed school. The highest support for single-sex schooling came from those in girls' schools with around a quarter to a third expressing this preference. The exception to this pattern is found in Wattle St. school where the boys have similar preferences for single-sex schooling to those in girls' schools. The preference for single-sex schooling does not vary systematically by other student characteristics.

Figure 4.4: Preference for single-sex schooling

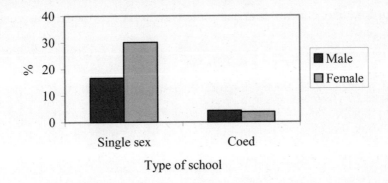

4.3 RELATIONS AMONG STUDENTS

In the group interviews, nearly all of the class groups in the case-study schools reported that the students in their class get on well together, with the exception of the class groups in Harris Street. Even though the majority of the class groups agree that generally their class gets on well together, they did recognise that some students may experience problems in getting on together:

> Interviewer: How would you say the students get on together in the school?
>
> Student: All right.
>
> Student: Might get some that don't mix well. (Park St. School, boys' school, middle stream class, mxc).

> Interviewer: How would you say students in second year get on with each other?
>
> Student: Grand.
>
> Student: A bit of slagging . . . but we don't hate each other. (Dawes Point School, boys' school, middle stream class, wc).

In Harris Street, a girls' school with a middle-class intake, the situation was very different, with the lack of mixing outside of existing friendship groups more evident than in any other of the case-study schools. Friendship cliques had formed within the student cohort quite early on in the junior cycle with some clashes between these groups and feelings of isolation among students who had 'fallen out' with their particular group of friends:

> Student: Like our class is all in groups.
>
> Student: Yeah, there's three or four groups in our class.
>
> Student: And like the second week in First Year like everybody got into groups.
>
> Student: Straightaway.
>
> Interviewer: So everyone kind of stays in their groups, do they?
>
> Student: Yeah.
>
> Student: I think that people only really get on with their friends. (Harris Street, Girls' school, mixed ability class, mc).

> Student: If you are stuck with a little group and say you start fighting with your friend then you can't really go off with anyone else because there is nobody else to go off with.
>
> Student: Yeah that is annoying.
>
> Student: Like you have to be friends with everyone . . . So that say I fell out with someone I could go over to [name] or whatever.
>
> Student: When I fell out with my friend I had nobody to go to so I had to end up sitting in the hall on my own again. (Harris Street, Girls' school, mixed ability class, mc).

In contrast, the majority of class groups across the other schools said that they mixed and socialised with students in other class groups; this was particularly evident in Argyle Street, Fig Lane and Lang Street:

> Interviewer: How would all the students get along with one another?
>
> Student: All grand, we're all friends, most of us hang around with each other, so I hang around with people from the top class and bottom class, all of them, we're all in clubs with each other as well, everyone knows each other. (Lang St. School, boys' school, middle stream class, wc).

It is not surprising that the students in Fig Lane are one of the schools to say that they more commonly mix with other class groups as the students in this school had all been regrouped into new base classes at the start of second year. The students believe this was a positive thing and helped them to get to know more students in the year:

> Student: Yeah, you have your own friends obviously outside class but then . . . if you're in a class you get on with the people in your class I think.
>
> Interviewer: Do you mix with anybody outside your class group?
>
> Student: Yeah, most of my friends are outside of my class, my good friends.
>
> Interviewer: Do you miss them at all that you are not in the same class group any longer?
>
> Student: No, not really, it's better to move class because you get to meet new people. (Fig Lane, Coed School, mixed ability class, mc).

> Interviewer: Do you mind that, that friends are kind of split up?
>
> Student: No because you'll make new ones and then you'll be just friends with more people and everything.
>
> Student: Yeah it's better than having a little group and never making new friends. (Fig Lane, Coed School, mixed ability class, mc).

Bullying was an issue that was raised by some of the class groups in the group interviews. Class groups in the case-study schools were divided in terms of whether they believe bullying is a problem in second year. Students in the class groups in six of the schools (Dawson Street, Barrack Street, Hay Street, Dawes Point, Belmore Street and Wattle Street) all said that bullying was not going on in second year:

> Student: No, it's not a bad school, there wouldn't really be any bullying. (Dawson Street, Coed School, mixed ability class, mxc).

> Student: No-one really gets bullied anyway so in this school, everyone's really friends with each other in the school. (Wattle Street, Boys' school, mixed ability class, mxc).

In contrast, students in Dixon Street, Park Street, Lang Street and Harris Street all feel that there is bullying taking place. Students generally do not define what types of bullying are taking place in the class although there is some evidence that groups from the girls' schools are more likely to mention verbal insults while groups in the boys' schools are more likely to talk about physical fights:

> Interviewer: Would they be like serious fights?
>
> Student: No.
>
> Student: They wouldn't be physical fights, they'd be like slagging.
>
> Student: They'd be slagging and saying stuff behind their backs.
>
> Student: People might be crying and stuff and go to a teacher, like sometimes it's gotten like really far in some classes where like people have gotten phone calls home and stuff.
>
> Student: Yeah and they'd be moved and stuff. (Harris Street, girls' school, mixed ability class, mc).

> Student: There was a fight a while ago and two people, they didn't want to fight but the class basically made them fight.
>
> Student: The whole school were cheering them on.
>
> Interviewer: And how can the class make them fight?
>
> Student: Well they'd insult them if they didn't.
>
> Student: They say they're going to fight and then they don't, they just call them chickens. (Park Street, boys' school, top stream class, mxc).

During the interviews with the class groups who spoke about bullying, nearly all of the class groups said that they thought students would probably not go to a teacher to report an incident of bullying:

> Interviewer: Just say if someone was being bullied do you think they'd go to a teacher about it?
>
> Three students at once: No.
>
> Interviewer: What would they do?
>
> Student: Just get on as normal.

Student: Fight back.

Student: Some people would go to teachers.

Interviewer: Does that work do you think if they go to the teachers?

Two students at once: No.

Interviewer: Why not?

Student: They stop for about a week and then they come back and start again. (Park St. School, boys' school, middle stream class, mxc).

Students in Harris Street School, where relations among students were perceived to be poor overall, spoke most openly about bullying and its prevalence across the class groups:

Interviewer: What kind of problems do you have?

Student: Screaming matches.

Student: Yeah.

Student: Bitching.

Student: Yeah.

Student: And everyone gets upset.

Student: It's just like girls are so horrible and then when you put loads of them together it's so much worse.

Student: Yeah.

Student: It's really bad in some situations.

Interviewer: And what kind of things would people be bitchy about?

Student: Judging people and laughing at things and then just talking about it after and then when everyone talks about it, it makes it so much worse.

Student: Yeah.

Student: And writing notes and other people finding them and stuff. (Harris St. School, girls' school, mixed ability class, mc).

This contrasted with the generally good class relations described by the students in Belmore Street School, another girls' school. Nearly all of the class groups in Belmore Street described themselves as the 'best class' in the year.

> Interviewer: How do you think students get on together in the school?
>
> Student: Fine.
>
> Student: Good.
>
> Student: Our class are good.
>
> Student: I think that [our class] is the nicest class and there is no bitchiness going on at all.
>
> Student: Everyone is good friends and even if you are not buddies you would still make the effort to say 'hi, how are you?' and chat. And say 'excuse me' and they do not bull pass you. (Belmore St. School, girls' school, mixed ability class, mxc).

The prevalence of bullying was explored in greater depth through the student questionnaires as students were expected to be more likely to report personal information about their experience of bullying outside a group setting. A number of different dimensions of bullying were considered, including being jeered or mocked, being physically pushed around, being bullied on the way to or from school, being upset by what others said and being upset because of being ignored by others. Among male students, being jeered or mocked was the most frequent form of bullying with over half of the students having experienced this behaviour in the previous two weeks (Figure 4.5). Among female students, being upset by things said behind their back, being jeered and being upset by being ignored were relatively similar in prevalence with around a third of female students experiencing these kinds of behaviours. Being physically pushed around by other students was less prevalent than verbal bullying but was twice as common among male as among female students.

Figure 4.5: Experience of being bullied (% one or more times)

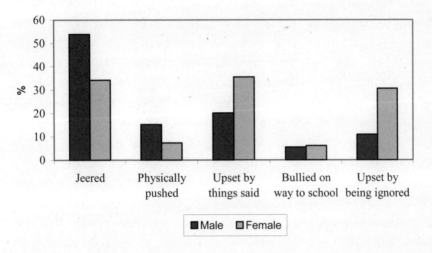

There is no significant difference by gender in the overall prevalence of bullying[4], but the forms of bullying vary by gender (see Figure 4.5). Students who rate themselves as 'below average' are more likely to report themselves as experiencing bullying than other students and, while the relationship with reading/maths scores is not marked, there is some evidence that girls with low ability test scores are more exposed to bullying. Students from minority backgrounds, newly arrived in Ireland or from the Traveller community, are significantly more likely to report having been bullied than other students, a pattern which is in keeping with that found among first year students (see Smyth et al., 2004). Experience of bullying is even more prevalent among immigrant students who had changed schools since first year, although this pattern should be interpreted with caution due to the small number of students involved. There is no significant difference across class types in the prevalence of being bullied. However, variation between schools is evident; the overall level of bullying, as well as the type of bullying encountered, is found to vary significantly across schools with the highest prevalence in Barrack St. school and the lowest levels found in Belmore St. school, both girls' schools. It is worth noting that Belmore St. was the only school to report dealing with bullying from a pastoral as well as a disciplinary perspec-

---

[4] A composite measure summarising all types of bullying has a reliability of 0.74.

tive (see Chapter Two). Generally, schools with more formalised support structures tend to have lower rates of bullying, though there is variation among these schools. The social mix of students in the school is not found to impact on bullying levels.

Of those who had experienced bullying, comparatively few students, under a third, had talked to someone about it. The most common sources of help were informal, mainly friends (65%), parents (55%) and siblings (15%), with telling school staff a relatively rare occurrence (teacher (12%) and Year Head (6%)). Overall, girls were much more likely to talk to someone about having been bullied than boys (46% compared with 17%). Over half of those who had experienced physical bullying, being bullied on the way to/from school or being upset by things said talked to someone about their experiences. There was significant variation across schools in the extent to which students talked to someone about their being bullied; the prevalence was lowest in Dawes Point and Park St. schools (both boys' schools) and highest in Belmore St. and Harris St. schools (both girls' schools). There was no evidence that students were more likely to talk to someone about being bullied when they attended schools with formalised support structures for second years.

4.4 DISCIPLINARY CLIMATE OF THE SCHOOL

Chapter Two discussed the involvement of key personnel, such as Year Heads and Class Tutors, in the disciplinary structures of the school. Information was collected in the student questionnaires on the extent of disruptive behaviour on the part of students. A third of students agreed with the statement that 'there are too many trouble-makers in my class' but the pattern of responses did not vary markedly across different groups of students. Within two of the streamed schools (Park St. and Dawes Point), students in the lower stream classes were more likely to report too many trouble-makers in their class than those in the higher stream classes.

Students were also asked about their own misbehaviour over the school year; variation across school contexts will not only reflect differences in the prevalence of misbehaviour but also different approaches to school discipline. A third of students had been absent from school more than six times in the course of second year[5] while 16 per cent of students had been late for school on more than six occasions (Figure 4.6). Almost half of the students surveyed had messed in class on three or more occasions while 17 per cent of students had skipped classes ('mitched'). In terms of punishment, a third had got into trouble for disobeying the school rules on three or more occasions. A quarter of students had done lines (3 or more times) as a punishment while a fifth had had to do extra homework. Fifteen per cent of students had done detention on three or more occasions while a tenth of students had been suspended on at least one occasion in the course of second year.

Figure 4.6: Prevalence of student misbehaviour

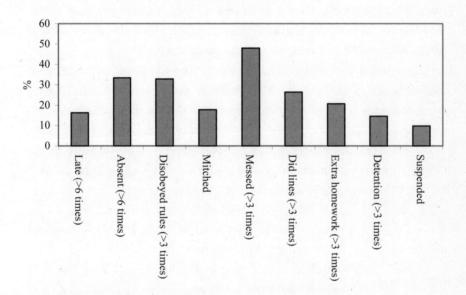

Differences were evident among groups of students in terms of the frequency of misbehaviour and related punishment. Female students were significantly less likely to record all forms of misbehaviour and punishment (except being absent from school). With the exception of being late for school and being absent for school, male students were more likely to

---

[5] Absenteeism will naturally reflect student illness as well as withdrawal from school. However, frequent absenteeism was found to be related to the other forms of misbehaviour.

report misbehaviour than female students in the same school. There was little systematic variation by social class background, although students from semi/unskilled manual or non-employed backgrounds were more likely to report having been suspended than students from other social class groups. To some extent, misbehaviour can be seen as both a reaction to, and a cause of, academic underperformance; students with lower reading and maths scores were more likely to engage in misbehaviour (with the exception of messing in class), a pattern which was particularly evident among boys. Within streamed schools, some forms of misbehaviour were more prevalent in lower stream classes. Being late for school, recurrent absenteeism, getting into trouble for disobeying the rules, doing detention or getting suspended were more common in lower stream than in higher stream classes. In contrast, 'messing' in class was somewhat more common in higher stream than in lower stream classes as were doing lines or extra homework as punishment.

A summary measure of misbehaviour, taking account of all forms of misbehaviour, was derived.[6] Misbehaviour is found to be significantly more common among male students and those from semi/unskilled manual backgrounds. Schools vary significantly in their levels of misbehaviour, reflecting the gender and socio-economic mix of students in the school; the highest levels of misbehaviour were found in Lang St. and Dixon St. schools, both designated disadvantaged schools which used streaming, and the lowest levels found in the three girls' schools. There was no clear relationship between the level of misbehaviour in a school and the existence of formalised support structures.

In the group interviews, students stressed the various discipline procedures and structures in the school. As indicated in Chapter Two, most discipline procedures are based on a record being made each time a student violates a school rule or misbehaves and after receiving a certain number of these 'marks', the student will receive detention; if the rule breaking continues and more 'marks' are given, the student may be suspended:

Interviewer: What happens if you get your name written down?

---

[6] This measure had a reliability of 0.82.

Student: Get your name written down three times you get a discipline entry

Interviewer: And what does that mean?

Student: . . . get three discipline entries you get a discipline meeting, get seven you're suspended. Get more than seven you're expelled. (Barrack St. School, girls' school, mixed ability class, wc).

Interviewer: If people are caught fighting what happens to them?

Student: I don't know.

Student: Three stages.

Student: Three stages and suspended.

Interviewer: So what's a stage?

Student: You get five of them and you're gone, I'm on my, I don't know how many now.

Student: You've about four, three or four.

Student: I've three.

Student: I don't know what I have.

Student: You've about four.

Student: I never got a stage in my life.

Student: [He] has four, how much have you got?

Student: None.

Student: You've about eight or nine.

Interviewer: I thought you said five and you're gone?

Student: Yeah, I know, they always keep saying you have them but I don't know.

Student: Five is your final one, once you have five then one more mistake after five and then you're gone. (Park St. School, boys' school, lower stream class, mxc).

It is commonly felt among second year students that the teachers are stricter than they were when the students were in first year, particularly in Park Street, Harris Street and Belmore Street:

It is a lot harder than first year and the teachers are more strict. (Belmore St. School, girls' school, mixed ability class, mxc)

[I]t's gotten stricter, since the beginning of last year, this year it's stricter, but years before it wasn't. (Park Street, Boys' school, middle stream, mxc)

Student: You get in more trouble.

Student: Yeah.

Student: In first year if you did something wrong like, it was just like ah well like, they didn't give you a detention or a mark but now like if you do anything bad like everyone gets detention or like a report or something.

Student: We used to get away with it but not anymore. (Harris Street, girls' school, mixed ability class, mc).

Although the students feel that in second year their teachers are stricter with them, this pattern does not apply across the board. Many students think that some teachers are stricter than others and, in keeping with the discussion of teacher 'favourites' above, some teachers were seen as inconsistent in disciplining students:

Student: Depends, there's some teachers that are very strict and then some that aren't and we have a strict year head. (Park Street, boys' school, higher stream, mxc).

Student: It depends, a teacher could like really like you and you could be a right pain in his class, tell you to stay quiet and everything but if he likes you he won't put you on detention or anything or if sometimes teachers put you on detention and then at the end of class ask you to come up and then they go now I'm not going to leave you on detention, you get very little detention. (Fig Lane, coed school, mixed ability class, mc).

Students generally see suspension as an ineffective punishment and most students report they would not mind being suspended from school as it simply means having time off from school to them:

Student: I don't think suspending you is a lot of good like to be honest because that's only giving you days off school like, that's what everyone wants. So like detention's worse because you have to stay in on Friday . . ., it's your playtime on Friday but like they suspend you and you just get off two days off school, but that's not really helping no one is it? You miss the schoolwork and all that. (Wattle St. School, boys' school, mixed ability class, mxc).

Interviewer: Do you think being suspended makes you change your behaviour?

Student: No.

Student: No.

Student: They're giving you days off. (Dawes Point School, boys' school, lower stream class, mxc).

There was also a strong feeling among some groups of students that teachers sometimes treated them unfairly and students got into trouble for things they hadn't done. This was most evident in Hay Street, Lang Street and Barrack Street schools, three schools with working-class intakes:

Student: Some people blink and they get lines, they get blamed for stuff, I'd say he could get lines now and it could be me that's doing it.

Student: You throw something at the blackboard when he's facing the blackboard and ... and he'll get up and he'll turn around and he'll just blame the first person he sees.

Student: The first person he looks at he'd blame. (Hay Street, coed school, middle/lower stream, wc).

Student: You feel like do something wrong, it will go round like teachers, but there's no point like you know, if you get a bad name, it's hard to get your good name back.

Student: They say things that are not true you know and just to get a bad name. . .

Student: Yeah they really do, don't think we're exaggerating saying that.

Student: They just give you [a] mention like when one person is like talking like the whole class gets mentioned, they used to do that the other day, she goes if you don't be quiet the whole class will get a discipline entry.

Student: Yeah it's not fair you know because teachers . . ., they shouldn't really . . . try to get you into trouble you know, that's what they do, they try to get you into trouble. (Barrack Street, girls' school, mixed ability class, wc).

However, similar claims were made by some student groups in other case-study schools with different student profiles:

Student: It's not that like, some people just listen to you and say okay what's wrong and but like this certain, that same teacher and another teacher just go okay it's both of your faults and you might have just been sitting there and they're like pounding you and you'd just be sitting there reading the book. And then she'll go okay yellow sheet, write out these two pages like. (Argyle Street, coed school, higher band, mxc).

In some schools, discipline problems are also seen to affect the students' ability to learn. In certain schools, particularly Dixon Street and Wattle Street (both designated disadvantaged schools), students felt that some-times they were suffering due to misbehaviour taking place in the class and the lack of control in some classes:

Student: The girls in our class are just ... throw chocolate and all at each other in the class.

Student: It's hard to learn. (Dixon Street, coed school, middle stream, wc).

Student: No, just the [subject] teacher has no control, she says she doesn't put us in detention because . . . she has to do detention with us when we mess and that so she kind of just lets us away with eve-rything.

Interviewer: Do you think that's a good idea?

Student: Well it's not such a good idea because like if we're allowed to mess you can't learn, so it's not gonna be handy for the Junior Cert. (Wattle Street, boys' school, mixed ability class, mxc).

In sum, the case-study schools are found to vary in the level of student misbehaviour as well as in the school's response to such behaviour. Generally, male students and those with lower academic ability levels have higher levels of misbehaviour. Schools serving greater concentrations of students from disadvantaged backgrounds tend to report more misbehaviour, a pattern which is seen as impacting on learning in the classroom by some students.

4.5 ENGAGEMENT IN SCHOOL LIFE

4.5.1 Attitudes to school

This section explores the extent to which students have positive attitudes to school and school life. The way in which student attitudes to school may have changed between first and second year is analysed in Chapter Six. As in first year (see Smyth et al., 2004), the majority of students have positive attitudes towards school in second year; they tend to be excited about school, like school and feel relaxed about school. Just over half find schoolwork interesting and look forward to coming to school while a third report liking school better than most other students (Figure 4.7). However, a certain group of students have more negative attitudes to school life with a significant proportion not finding schoolwork interesting.

A composite measure of liking school[7] indicates differences among groups of students in their overall attitudes to school. Female students tend to be more positive about school than their male counterparts, a pattern which is also evident within coed schools (though with a narrow gender gap in Dixon St. school). The variation by family background is not significant but those from farming and professional background have somewhat more positive attitudes to school as do students newly arrived in Ireland. Students from a Traveller background are found to have more negative attitudes to school overall. Students with lower reading/maths scores tend to have somewhat more negative attitudes to school but the differences by ability are not marked. The most positive attitudes to school are found among those in mixed ability and higher stream classes

---

[7] This measure has a reliability of 0.81.

with the least positive attitudes found among those in lower stream classes. There is significant variation in attitudes to school across the case-study schools. On the whole, the existence of formalised support structures does not necessarily facilitate more positive attitudes to school. Attitudes to school tend to be more negative in working-class schools but there is variation among these schools, with very positive attitudes among students in Hay St. school, for example.

Figure 4.7: Liking school

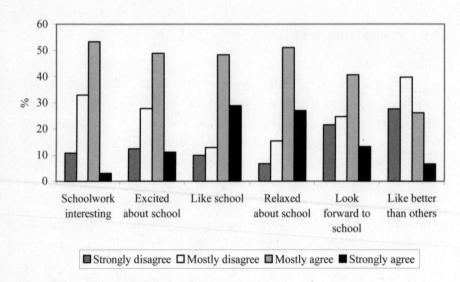

4.5.2 Attitudes to teachers

As well as being positive about their school, second year students tend to be positive about their teachers, finding them friendly and feeling they would help with a schoolwork-related problem (Figure 4.8). However, around a third of students do not like most of their teachers, do not feel they could talk to them if they had a problem and do not consider there is a good atmosphere in their class.

On a composite measure of liking teachers[8], female students are more likely to report liking their teachers, with gender differences evi-

---

[8] This measure has a reliability of 0.79.

dent within coed schools (although with a narrower gender gap in Fig Lane school). There are no significant differences in liking teachers by social class background of the student. Students newly arrived in Ireland have somewhat more positive attitudes, and Traveller students less positive attitudes, to teachers but the differences between groups are not statistically significant. Attitudes to teachers are most positive in mixed ability and lower stream classes and least positive in higher stream classes. Furthermore, attitudes to teachers vary significantly across the case-study schools; they tend to be somewhat more positive in schools with formalised support structures (such as Hay St., Harris St. and Belmore St.) and less positive in schools with a concentration of working-class students (such as Lang St. school).

Figure 4.8: Liking teachers

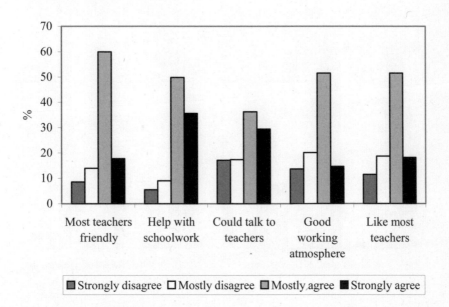

4.5.3 Student isolation/anxiety

In general, around a tenth of students appear to feel isolated within their school context – being scared by school, feeling ignored, feeling alone and not having many friends (Figure 4.9). Furthermore, a third of students report feeling down about their life at times while over a quarter are afraid of making a fool of themselves in class and are afraid to tell teachers if they do not understand something.

Female students are more likely to report feelings of isolation[9] than their male counterparts, a pattern which is evident within coed schools (with the exception of Argyle St. school). However, there is no variation in reported isolation by students' social class background. Students from minority ethnic groups, newly arrived in Ireland or from the Traveller community, are more likely to report feeling isolated in school, in keeping with the higher levels of bullying they experience (see above). Feelings of isolation are highest in mixed ability and higher stream classes and (for male students) lowest in lower stream classes. The variation in reported isolation by school is not significant but levels are somewhat higher in two of the girls' schools (Barrack St. and Harris St.). The pattern for Barrack St. is likely to reflect the high levels of bullying there while students in Harris St. tended to report very rigid friendship cliques within the school.

Figure 4.9: Isolation

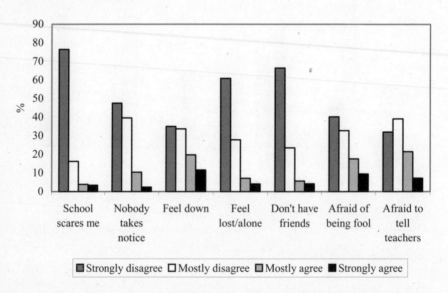

Students' attitudes to school and school life are found to be inter-related; students who have positive attitudes to school tend to have positive atti-

---

[9] This measure has a reliability of 0.76.

tudes to teachers and are less likely to feel isolated within school. Students' feelings of isolation are found to be related to the social climate of the school; those who feel isolated are more likely to have been bullied and less likely to have had positive interaction with teachers. Similarly, attitudes to school are found to be influenced by the school's social climate; as might be expected, those who have had positive interaction with teachers are more likely to like school and teachers while those who have had negative interaction with teachers are less likely to like school and teachers. Students who like school and teachers also tend to have more positive self-images, especially more positive perceptions of their academic abilities (see below).

4.5.4 Student disaffection

There was evidence from the group interviews of some students becoming detached and disaffected with school life in certain school contexts. Some students reported being eager to finish school; the issue of educational aspirations in general and early school leaving in particular is discussed in Chapter Five. Students in the lower stream classes interviewed were much more likely to say they would leave school before they attained their Leaving Certificate and possibly even before the Junior Certificate:

Interviewer: Are you going to take Junior Cert exams?

Student: I amn't, no.

Student: No.

. . .

Interviewer: How long are you going to stay in the school do you think?

Student: Next month.

Student: Until third year.

Interviewer: Okay, so what happens in the third year, are you going to leave?

Student: Yeah.

Interviewer: Okay, and what are you going to do then?

Student: Don't know. (Dixon St. School, coed school, lower stream class, wc).

Disaffection was seen to impact not only on potential early school leaving but on school attendance. Although the students who themselves participated in the group interviews in Barrack Street, a designated disadvantaged school, did not appear to be particularly disengaged with school life, these students revealed that there were other students in their class who were regularly absent from school:

Interviewer: Would there be people staying out of school much?

Student: Yeah.

Student: Yeah some people do.

Student: I don't stay out much like.

Student: Like there's these girls in the class that like you don't see them for two months.

Interviewer: So some people when they don't turn up it's not because they're sick is it?

Student: No.

Student: They just make up excuses and everything, just they're somewhere else. (Barrack Street, girls' school, mixed ability class, wc).

Many classes in the group interviews expressed the view that they are uninterested in school and school life and have effectively disengaged themselves from their schoolwork. These classes were almost exclusively the lower stream classes in streamed schools, namely, Dixon Street, Park Street, Hay Street, Lang Street and Dawes Point; four of these schools also had predominantly working-class student intakes. Dixon St. School students appeared to be the most disaffected with school:

Interviewer: Is there anybody in your class that actually like learning?

Student: No.

Student: This is a dumb ass school. (Dixon St. School, coed school, lower stream class, wc) .

Student disaffection was also reflected in the lack of time spent on homework, an issue which is discussed further in Chapter Five. In keeping with the teacher accounts in Chapter Three, students in lower stream classes reported getting very little homework but tended not to do the homework that was set for them:

Interviewer: So how much homework would you get this year?

Student: Very, very little.

Student: Yeah.

Student: Doesn't matter, I don't do it.

Interviewer: How much time would you spend on it?

Student: Ten minutes.

Student: Not even ten minutes.

Student: I'll be honest with you I don't do it at all.

Student: Couldn't be bothered.

Student: We don't get much, we only get one thing so we don't bother doing it. (Park Street, Boys' School, lower stream, mxc).

The frustration with school life experienced by some students is vividly captured in the following quote, which indicates a growing tension between these students and the structures of school:

Student: School drives you mad, it actually would, the teachers, if you'd better teachers there would be no one getting in trouble.

Student: When you come back at the start of the year you're alright for a while.

. . .

Student: You calm down but then it starts building up through the year because you're so bored of school and you want to get out of it. (Lang St. School, boys' school, middle stream class, wc).

4.5.5 Student involvement in the school

Students were asked about their level of involvement in extra-curricular and non-school social activities. Two-thirds of students in the case-study schools had some involvement in school-based sports in the two weeks prior to the survey while three quarters were involved in sports outside school. By contrast, only a minority (37%) of students were involved in other extracurricular activities (such as school clubs, groups, plays or debates) while the majority (83%) had taken part in social activities out-side school such as discos, concerts or the cinema (Figure 4.10).

Figure 4.10: Student involvement in school and non-school social activities

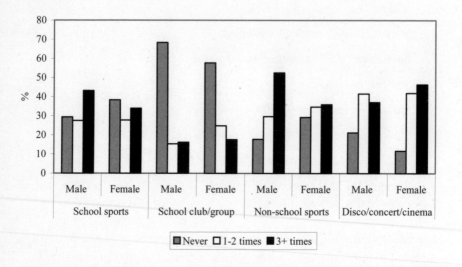

Clear gender differences were apparent among second year students, with male students being much more likely to be involved in sports whether school-based or outside school.[10] When male and female students in the same school are considered, there is no variation in patterns of participation in school-based sports but persistent gender differences emerge in relation to non-school sports (except in the case of Argyle St. school). Female students were more likely than their male counterparts to be involved in other extracurricular activities. With the exception of Dixon St. school, female students are more likely to be involved in other extracurricular activities than male students in the same school. There is no consistent evidence that more academically able students are more (or

---

[10] Interestingly, gender disparities are even more marked in relation to non-school sports than to school sports.

less) involved in sports and extracurricular activities. However, students with lower reading and maths scores tend to have a more active social life outside school, perhaps indicating they have already begun a process of disengaging from schoolwork as their main focus.

Within streamed schools, students in lower stream classes are somewhat less likely than those in higher stream classes to be involved in school sports. In contrast, students in lower stream classes tend to have a more active social life than those in higher or mixed ability classes. Involvement in school sports varies across schools but appears to be related to more general school ethos regarding sport rather than the gender or social profile of the students. Variation across schools in extracurricular activities is not marked although involvement is somewhat higher in Barrack St. school, a girls' school, and lower in Park St. school, a boys' school.

4.6 STUDENT SELF-IMAGE

4.6.1 Academic self-image

A number of different aspects of student self-image were considered in this study, including academic self-image (student perceptions of their own academic abilities) as well as body-image and perceptions of their popularity and efficacy at sports. Second year students in the case-study schools tend to have a broadly positive view of their own academic abilities. The majority of students feel they are doing well at school, are working hard, are as able as others and are pleased with their schoolwork (Figure 4.11). Around half of the students feel they do better at schoolwork than most other students in their class. However, some students appear to be experiencing difficulties. Almost half of students do not find the work quite easy at school and almost a quarter report difficulties keeping up with their schoolwork.

Figure 4.11: Academic self-image

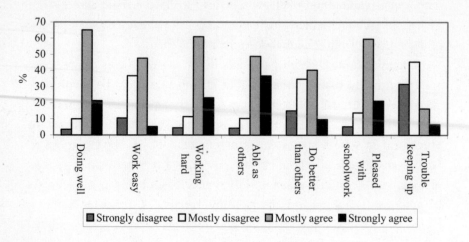

There are no significant gender differences in a composite measure of academic self-image[11], that is, in students' perceived capacity to cope with their schoolwork. Students from professional or farming backgrounds tend to rate their abilities more positively than other students. In contrast, students from Traveller backgrounds are less positive about their abilities. As might be expected, students with higher reading and maths scores in first year are more likely to have positive views of their capacity to manage their schoolwork. This relationship is stronger for reading than for maths scores, most likely reflecting the strong language and literacy base to many junior cycle subjects. Interestingly, there are no significant differences by class type in perceived academic abilities; this may relate to the fact that students are comparing themselves to students in their own class when assessing how well they are doing at school. Similarly, there are no significant differences across schools in academic self-image, again indicating the 'frog pond' effect where students compare themselves with their peers rather than to a more global standard.

---

[11] This measure has a reliability of 0.81.

Figure 4.12: Rating in relation to class and year

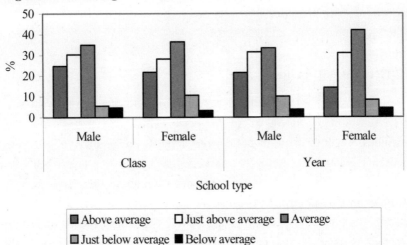

Two other measures of academic self-image were examined: students' self-rating at tests/exams in relation to their class and in relation to students in their year. Only a small proportion of students consider themselves 'just below average' or 'below average' in relation to tests or exams (Figure 4.12). Male students are more likely to consider themselves 'above average' than female students, a pattern which contrasts with the lack of gender differences found when students were asked about their ability to cope with their schoolwork (see above). Within coed schools, male students tend to be more likely to think they are above average in their class. Students from farming and professional backgrounds are more likely to rate themselves as above average in both their class and year group than other students. Self-perceptions reflect actual performance differences with students with lower reading/maths scores more likely to rate themselves as below average. However, variation is evident between students with similar scores, indicating a more complex social relationship at play.

Students in lower stream classes are more likely to rate themselves as average in their class than other students. As might be expected, the pattern for rating in relation to the year group is more strongly differentiated by class type with 34 per cent of those in higher stream classes rating themselves as above average compared with 18 per cent in mixed ability classes. As might be expected, students' perceived ability to cope with their school work is significantly related to how students rate themselves in relation to their class and year group.

4.6.2 General self-image

Three other aspects of self-image were explored among second year students: body-image, rating of sports performance and popularity with classmates. On the whole, second year students are positive about their appearance. However, there are marked differences by gender with female students being significantly more negative about their appearances than their male counterparts (Figure 4.13), a pattern which holds within coed schools (see also Hannan et al., 1996). Students from professional backgrounds have more negative body-images than other students. Male students in middle or lower stream classes, tend to have more positive body-images but there is little variation across class type for girls. Students in predominantly working-class schools, especially girls, tend to have somewhat more positive body-images than those in mixed or middle-class schools.

Figure 4.13: Body-image ('I like the way I look')

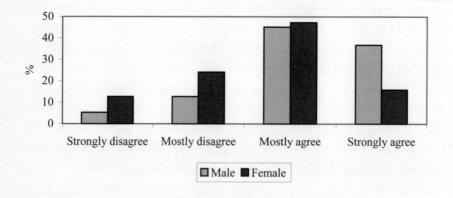

Figure 4.14: 'Good at sports'

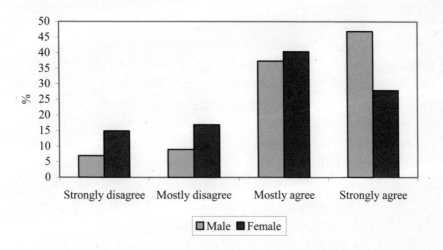

Male students in the surveyed schools are significantly more likely to report that they are good at sports than their female counterparts (Figure 4.14). This pattern applies within coed schools with the exception of Argyle St. school (a pattern which is probably due to the absence of gender differentiation in participation in non-school sports in this school). There is no significant difference in perceived ability at sport by parental background. Boys with lower reading/maths scores tend to have more positive views of their sports abilities, perhaps indicating that sports compensate for more negative experiences within school.

The vast majority (89%) of second year students see themselves as popular with their classmates. There are no significant differences in this perception by gender. Students from minority groups, those newly arrived in Ireland as well as those from Traveller backgrounds, describe themselves as less popular with their classmates; these patterns are consistent with the reported prevalence of bullying of these minority groups.

Body-image, sports self-image and perceived popularity are positively inter-correlated, that is, students who have a positive opinion of their appearance tend to think they are good at sport and popular with their classmates. Academic self-image is also positively related to the other aspects of self-image, indicating that some students appear to be more self-confident across a range of different aspects of their personality. Student self-image appears to be responsive to the social climate of the school. Students who have experienced bullying have more negative self-images across all four dimensions, that is, they have more negative views of their appearance, their academic abilities, their sporting ability and their popularity. Students who have experienced positive interaction with teachers tend to have more positive self-images, both academic and social. Students who have experienced negative interaction with teachers are more negative about their academic abilities. However, they are somewhat more positive about their sporting abilities and popularity. There are some differences between girls and boys in the relationships between different aspects of student self-image. Girls who are academically oriented also describe themselves as being good at sports, popular with their classmates and report good relations with their teachers. In contrast, some boys who report being popular have negative relations with their teachers; they would appear to pursue popularity with their classmates by 'playing the clown' or otherwise misbehaving in class.

4.7 CONCLUSIONS

This chapter has discussed variation across the case-study schools in their informal climate, that is, in the quality of relations between teachers and students and among students themselves. Variation is also evident within schools, with lower stream classes reporting more positive *and* more negative interaction with teachers than other class groups. This pattern appears to reflect, in part, the smaller class sizes for lower stream groups with more individual attention to students. However, in spite of greater contact with teachers, students in lower stream classes tended to characterise their relations with teachers as negative and were more likely to report disaffection with school-life.

While students indicated that they would approach (at least some) teachers in relation to a schoolwork-related problem, there was a general reluctance among students to say they would approach school personnel about a more personal problem. Where students had actually been bullied, for example, very few of them had talked to anyone in the school about it and were more reliant on family and friends in dealing with the issue. Having more developed support structures in the school did not guarantee more positive interaction between teachers and students or teachers being seen as more approachable by students, indicating the importance of the informal climate of the school in enhancing student access to support.

In general, second year students in the case-study schools had positive attitudes to school life. However, attitudes were somewhat less positive among male students and among those in lower stream classes. Students' perceptions of school were strongly related to the school climate, that is, to the quality of relations with teachers and other students.

APPENDIX 4.1: COMPONENTS
OF ATTITUDES SCALES

Scale	Items
Positive teacher-student interaction	You have been told your work is good by a teacher. You have asked questions in class. A teacher has praised you for answering a question. You have been asked questions in class by the teacher. You have been praised by a teacher because your written work is well done.
Negative teacher-student interaction	You have been given out to by a teacher because your work is untidy or not done on time. You have been given out to by a teacher for misbehaving in class.
Perceptions of unequal treatment of students	Teachers in this school treat the different classes in second year differently. Teachers in this school don't have students who are favourites. Teachers in this school treat hardworking students the best. Teachers treat students who come from Ireland better than those who have come from abroad. Teachers in this school treat the cleverest students the best. Boys and girls are treated equally by teachers in this school.

Being bullied	You have been jeered or mocked by other students.
	You have been bullied by being physically pushed around by other students.
	You have been upset by things said behind your back by other students.
	You have been pestered or bullied on the way to or from school.
	You have been upset by other students ignoring you.
Misbehaviour	I was late for school.
	I was absent from school (for any reason).
	I got into trouble for not following school rules.
	I skipped classes or mitched.
	I messed in class.
	I had to do lines as punishment.
	I had to do extra homework as punishment.
	I had to do detention (after school or at lunchtime).
	I was suspended from school.
Liking school	I find school-work in this school really interesting.
	I am excited about being at this school.
	I like being at this school.
	I usually feel relaxed about school.
	I look forward to coming to school most days.
	I like school better than most other students in this school.
Liking teachers	I think most of my teachers are friendly.
	My teachers would help me if I had a problem with my school work.
	I could talk to at least one of my teachers if I had a problem.
	Most of the time there is a good working atmosphere in the class.
	I like most of my teachers.

Isolation/anxiety	Being at this school scares me. Nobody at this school seems to take any notice of me. At times I feel down about my life. I don't have many friends at this school. I'm afraid that I'll make a fool of myself in class. I am afraid to tell teachers when I don't understand something.
Student involvement	Taken part in sports in your school outside class time Taken part in sports not organised by this school Taken part in a club, debate, music group or play organised by the school outside class time Been to a disco, concert or the cinema
Academic self-image	I think I am doing well at this school. I think the work is quite easy at this school. I think I am working hard at this school. I am able to do my school-work as well as most other students. I do better at school-work than most other students in my class. I'm quite pleased with how my school-work is going. I have trouble keeping up with my school-work.

Chapter Five

STUDENT PERSPECTIVES ON TEACHING AND LEARNING

Chapter Four explored student perceptions of the social climate of the school, including their relations with teachers and their peers. This chapter looks in greater detail at students' experiences of teaching and learning in second year. The first section explores the identity of second year students as learners, contrasting their experiences in second year with those in first year. The second section examines students' perceptions of effective teachers and teaching methods while student views on what helps them learn are discussed in section three. The fourth section looks at student attitudes to learning, including the way in which such attitudes are influenced by their peer group. Sections five and six look at homework and support for learning offered within the school. Section seven discusses student views on subject choice and their attitudes to specific subject areas; the extent to which student attitudes have changed since first year will be explored in Chapter Six. The final section looks at student orientations to the future in terms of the Junior Certificate exam and their longer term educational and career aspirations.

5.1 BEING IN SECOND YEAR

5.1.1 Comparing first and second year: Difficulty of schoolwork

Students were asked to compare their experiences in second year with those in first year. Students were almost equally divided between finding schoolwork in second year harder and finding it about the same. Only a very small proportion (6%) reported that schoolwork had become easier over time. Female students were more likely than their male counterparts to report that second year was harder (51% compared with 45%). However, this was due to the gender distribution across schools with no significant differences apparent between girls and boys in the same school. Those from professional backgrounds were somewhat more likely to find schoolwork harder. There is some variation by academic self-rating; students who report themselves as doing below average in tests/exams compared to their year group are more likely to find schoolwork harder but a significant proportion of them find schoolwork easier. However, in terms of actual ability levels, students with lower reading and maths scores are likely to find schoolwork easier while those with higher scores are more likely to find it harder. Students from a Traveller background are somewhat more likely to report finding schoolwork in second year harder as are students who had changed schools since first year.

Figure 5.1: Comparison of second year and first year in relation to schoolwork and homework

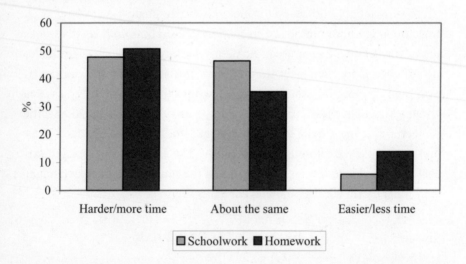

Class type is significantly related to experiences in second year; those in mixed ability classes are more likely to find schoolwork harder, those in higher stream classes are equally split between 'harder' and 'about the same' while those in middle and lower stream classes are most likely to report 'about the same' but with more than a tenth finding schoolwork easier. The pattern of responses varies significantly across the case-study schools and in general students in predominantly working-class schools are likely to find schoolwork 'about the same' rather than 'harder'.

5.1.2 Comparing first and second year: Time spent on homework

Half of the students surveyed felt that they spent more time on homework in second year than in first year; over a third felt they spent about the same amount of time while 14 per cent reported spending less time (Figure 5.1). Subsequent analyses will explore actual changes between first and second year in the amount of time spent on homework. Female students were more likely to report spending more time on homework (57% compared with 45%) and less likely to report doing less homework (10% compared with 17%) than their male counterparts. This pattern is not solely related to the gender distribution across schools as, within co-educational schools, girls report spending more time on homework; the exception to this pattern occurs in Dixon St. school. Students from professional, other non-manual and farming backgrounds were more likely to report spending more time on homework with the highest proportions spending less time found among those from semi/unskilled manual backgrounds. The pattern is associated with ability level and academic self-rating; students with higher reading and maths scores in first year are likely to be spending more time on homework in second year while students who deem themselves 'below average' and/or have lower ability levels tend to spend less time on homework.

Class type is significantly related to the amount of time spent on homework; those in mixed ability classes reported spending more time, those in higher/middle classes were equally divided between 'more time' and 'about the same' while those in lower stream classes were more likely than any other group to spend less time on homework (28% compared with 12% for top classes). The pattern varies significantly across the case-study schools; students in mixed or middle-class schools (such as Argyle St. and Fig Lane) are more likely to spend more time on homework while those in working-class schools (such as Hay St. and Dawes Point) are most likely to spend less time on homework.

Overall, in comparing second and first year experiences, two groups of students are evident: those for whom second year represents an intensification of their academic engagement and workload, and those who are 'drifting' or, in some cases, disengaging in terms of schoolwork. The first group is made up disproportionately of female students, those from professional, other non-manual and farming backgrounds, those with higher prior academic ability and those in mixed ability or higher stream classes. In contrast, the second group is disproportionately made up of those from lower stream classes, those with lower ability levels, those who rate their academic abilities as below average and those from working-class backgrounds. It is clear, therefore, that important differentiation processes in orientation to schoolwork appear to be taking place in second year.

5.1.3 Comparing first and second year: Student views

The comparison between second and first year was explored in greater depth in the group interviews with students. The responses from the students in the group interviews were very similar to the responses in the questionnaire in terms of how the students feel about schoolwork and homework in second year. Generally students feel that schoolwork in second year is harder than it was in first year:

> Student: We have to work harder because we have to go to third year and do our Leaving and Junior Certs. (Barrack St. School, girls' school, mixed ability class, wc).

> Student: It's a lot harder . . . 'cause in First Year you're just getting used to it and you're just getting into the school . . . and you get more homework and you have to study more as well. (Wattle St. School, boys' school, mixed ability class, mxc).

Although many of the class groups feel that schoolwork is harder in second year compared to first year, some class groups do feel that having fewer subjects in second year helps to make schoolwork a little easier. Students in Argyle Street and Belmore Street, both schools that had taster programmes in first year, were most likely to express this opinion:

Student: It is sometimes . . . harder but your subjects are reduced so you can focus on the subjects that you picked. So in a way it is harder but it is less stress because you do not have the ones that you dropped. (Belmore Street, girls' school, mixed ability class, mxc).

Student: There's a lot less option subjects, you know, I only have to pick two out of like eight or something, so there's a lot less books and stuff to be carrying around.

Interviewer: Ok, is it a good thing or a bad thing?

Student: It's a good thing because you're kind of more focused on the subjects then. (Argyle Street, coed school, mixed ability, mxc).

Some class groups do feel that schoolwork is about the same as in the previous year; these responses were most prevalent in two of the working-class schools (Dixon Street and Hay Street) but also in Dawson Street school, a school with a mixed student intake:

Interviewer: How is like the schoolwork compared to first year?

Student: It's a bit different like

Student: It's the same.

Interviewer: Okay, and you said a bit different?

Student: It's the same but it's harder. (Dixon Street, coed School, lower stream, wc).

A small minority of students feel that the schoolwork is actually easier in second year. The reasons for this are varied. In Dawson Street and Hay Street, some students feel that the schoolwork is just generally easier. Students in two of the streamed boys' schools, Park Street and Dawes Point, also report finding schoolwork easier. Within the streamed schools, there appear to be two countervailing reasons behind student perceptions of schoolwork being easier. On the one hand, students in the higher stream groups felt that teachers had put a good deal of pressure on them in first year but that pressure had lessened somewhat in second year:

Student: The school work is easier for some reason.

Student: Yeah.

Student: It's because the teachers were just trying to push us to see what they could get out of you in first year and this year they know what you're up to.

Student: They know what you're like.

Student: They know what your level of achievement is. (Dawes Point, boys' school, higher stream, wc).

On the other hand, some students in the lower streams felt schoolwork was easier because they had disengaged from active involvement: 'Sure we don't do any work . . . it's easier' (Dawes Point, lower stream, bs mxc). Familiarity with subjects was also seen as making second year somewhat easier:

Student: Sort of easier because the work gets sort of easier as well.

Student: The first year is like all new stuff.

Student: Yeah, the material and the subjects are so new to you in first year that like in second year you're used to it, so it becomes easier. (Park St. School, boys' school, middle stream, mxc).

The pattern for homework is identical to that for schoolwork. Those who say that schoolwork has got harder in second year compared to first year also say that they are getting more homework and that it is harder. Those who find schoolwork about the same find homework about the same as first year. Interestingly, those who find schoolwork easier generally did not mention homework. Most of the class groups say that they find they are getting more homework in second year compared to first year and that the homework has also become harder:

Student: There's more homework, you get more homework and the work is harder. (Fig Lane, coed School, mixed ability class, mc).

Student: You get more homework and they teach you now about the Junior Cert and different subjects in second year.

Student: You have to do more work.

Student: You have to do much more homework and study a lot. (Dawson St. School, coed class, mixed ability class, mxc).

In terms of interaction with teachers, students talked a lot about how teachers were stricter in second year compared to first year; this was evident across a range of schools with different gender and social mixes (for example, Argyle Street, Barrack Street, Harris Street, Fig Lane and one class group in Lang Street):

> Interviewer: If you compare how the teachers treated you last year and how they treat you this year, is there any difference?
>
> Student: Yeah last year they were a bit more relaxed, well not relaxed but they weren't as strict.
>
> Student: They knew that we were new to the school and that everything couldn't be perfect in a week after just coming into a new school.
>
> Student: It just shows you that some of them just have this thing in their head like first years treat them nice, second years don't. (Fig Lane School, coed school, mixed ability class, mc).

> Student: When we were in first year you got away with everything,
>
> Student: . . . I think the reason why we got away with everything in first year is because like we were only like new to the school.
>
> Student: So now . . . we're used to the school so they're going a bit stricter. (Barrack St. School, girls' school, mixed ability class, wc).

Although many students felt schoolwork more difficult in second year and spent more time on homework, they also referred to feeling more settled into the school in contrast to the adjustments they had to make in first year:

> Student: In first year you're just getting to know the school, in second year you're used to it. (Dixon St. School, coed school, middle stream, mxc).

> Student: And like second year is better because you know the girls in your class much better, so like it is easier (Belmore St. School, girls' school, mixed ability class, mxc).

> Student: But you're more sort of settled in from first year

Student: More settled in, things like that. (Barrack St. School, girls'
school, mixed ability class, wc).

5.1.4 Comparisons with primary school

Second year students were also asked to refer back to their primary
school experiences in terms of whether they would prefer to be back in
primary school and the degree to which they miss their friends from primary school. In keeping with analyses of transition difficulties among
first year students (Smyth et al., 2004), the majority (77%) of students
disagree with the statement that 'I wish I could have stayed at my primary school'. However, it is noteworthy that 23 per cent of students
agree with this statement indicating some longer term difficulties in adjustment to post-primary education. Students who reported some difficulties tended to be disproportionately girls with lower reading scores,
those from semi/unskilled manual backgrounds, and those who rated
themselves as below average. The pattern varies significantly by school
with the highest levels agreeing in Barrack St. and Lang St. schools, both
designated disadvantaged schools.

Somewhat surprising is the relatively large proportion (40%) of students who continue to miss their friends from primary school, even towards the end of second year. Female students are much more likely to
report missing their primary school friends than their male counterparts
(22% strongly agree compared with 11%), a pattern which is evident
within coed schools. Missing primary school friends is also somewhat
more common among those from semi/unskilled manual backgrounds
and those who changed schools since first year. The pattern varies significantly by school with the highest proportions agreeing in Barrack St.
and Harris St. schools, both girls' schools.

In sum, for many students second year represents an intensification
of their school workload. Although the workload may be heavier, this
appears to be partially compensated for by the fact that students have
grown more accustomed to the school structures and are more socially
integrated into the school. However, it is worth noting that some students
experience longer term difficulties in settling into post-primary education; this is especially evident among working-class students and/or
those who see their academic abilities as below average. A significant

group of female students are also likely to report missing their primary school friends, even towards the end of second year.

5.2 PERCEPTIONS OF TEACHERS AND TEACHING

5.2.1 Pace of instruction

This section explores student perceptions of the pace of instruction in their class as well as their views on what makes for effective teaching. A considerable proportion of second year students were dissatisfied with the pace of instruction in their lessons; twenty-eight per cent of the students felt that their teachers went too slowly with their class while thirty per cent felt that teachers went too quickly (Figure 5.2). There are no marked differences by gender or social class background in student perceptions of the pace of instruction. Students who rate themselves as below average are more likely than other students to think that teachers go too quickly with their class (58% of those below average compared with 19% of those above average) as are those with lower reading and maths scores. Students in lower stream classes are most likely to feel that teachers go too slowly (49% compared with 21% of those in higher stream classes and 24% of those in mixed ability classes). Interestingly, there is no significant variation across class types in the proportion of students who feel that teachers go too quickly with their class. On the whole, students in predominantly working-class schools (such as Barrack St. and Lang St.) are more likely to think that their teachers go too quickly with their class. However, the effect of streaming in many working-class schools (for example, Dixon St.) meant that student responses were polarised with lower streams reporting that teachers go too slowly and higher streams reporting that teachers go too quickly.

Students were also asked about the pace of instruction in specific subject classes. In general, the majority of second year students felt that the teacher went at about the right speed in class; students were somewhat more satisfied with the pace of instruction in English than in the other specified subjects (Figure 5.3). With the exception of English, students were more likely to think that the teacher went too quickly rather than too slowly with their class. Over a quarter of students found this to be the case in Maths, Science and French while over a fifth found this to be the case in German, History and Geography. More than a tenth of students reported their teachers went too slowly with their class; this was less prevalent in Maths and French than in the other subjects.

Figure 5.2: Student perceptions of pace of instruction

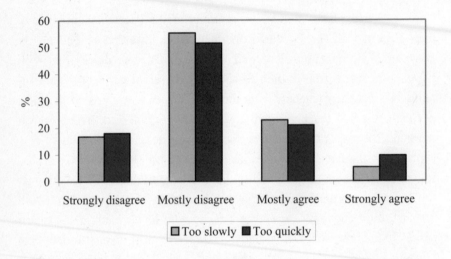

Some differences were evident between groups of students in their perceptions of the pace of instruction in specific subject areas. Students who considered themselves below average in their year group were significantly more likely to report that teachers went too quickly in all of the specified subjects; a relatively high proportion of 'below average' students had particular problems with the pace of instruction in French and German. In contrast, students who rated themselves as above average in their year group were significantly more likely to consider that their teachers went too slowly in English, French and Geography. In general, students with lower prior ability levels felt that pace of instruction was too fast in the languages (English, French and German) as well as in History. There was significant variation across schools and class groups, though the pattern differed for the specific subject areas.

Figure 5.3: Pace of instruction by subject

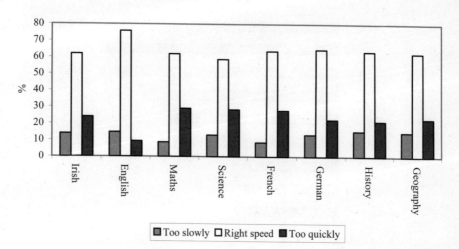

5.2.2 Effective teaching

Students were asked about the teacher characteristics that helped them to learn best. Teachers explaining things was seen as very important by three-quarters of the second year students surveyed (Figure 5.4). The majority of students also saw teachers enjoying teaching the subject, being able to talk to teachers and being able to have a laugh with teachers as very important qualities. Over forty per cent of students saw encouraging students to ask questions in class and praising students for good work as very important. Not giving out to students, keeping order in class and relating lessons to life outside school were seen as somewhat less important teacher qualities in enhancing student learning.

There was some variation across groups of students in their views on effective teachers. Female students tend to mention a wide range of teacher characteristics as important while male students are more likely than female students to see teachers who don't give out to you as important. Students who rate themselves as below average and those with lower reading/maths scores are also more likely to see teachers not giving out as important. Students from professional backgrounds are more likely to see relating lessons to life as important. Differences in views on effective teaching were also evident across the case-study schools.

Figure 5.4: Teacher characteristics (% 'very important')

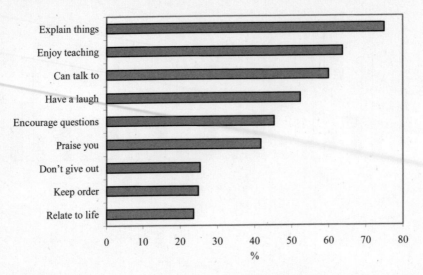

Twenty-nine per cent of the students saw all of the teacher qualities listed as important or very important. However, only one of the students saw none of the characteristics as important so there is no evidence that disaffected students consider there are no ways in which teachers could make a difference.

Students in the group interviews also spoke about what they thought were the qualities and behaviour of a good teacher. As in the question-naire responses, the single frequently mentioned aspect was the teachers' ability to explain the subject or topic to the students:

> Interviewer: And thinking about your teachers this year, what do you think makes a good teacher?

> Student: If they explain well, and if you ask them again that they do not mind explaining it again. (Belmore Street, girls' school, mixed ability class, mxc).

Being able to have a laugh with the teacher or being able to have fun in class emerged as very important qualities in a number of schools:

> Student: Doesn't roar at you.

> Student: Yeah and you can have a laugh with them and all.

Student: . . . There's teachers where you can do your work and they mess with you, and there's teachers who really shout at you if you say something in the class. (Dixon Street, coed school, lower stream, wc).

Student: Like a teacher that can be strict but you can get on with them.

Student: Yeah you can have a bit of craic.

Student: You can talk in class or can ask questions.

Student: Because if a teacher is strict you might be afraid to ask them questions but if you can have a bit of craic with them then you wouldn't. (Dawson St. School, coed school, mixed ability class, mxc).

Students also discussed the characteristics of a bad teacher. In these discussions, students often focused on describing individual teachers but a number of general characteristics did emerge. Firstly, teachers who did not explain things in class were seen in negative terms, especially if this was combined with too fast a pace of instruction or too heavy a workload:

Interviewer: What do you think makes a bad teacher?

Student: They rush and they do not explain things (Belmore St. School, girls' school, mixed ability class, mxc).

Student: Gives you too much and doesn't tell you enough about what you're doing. (Dawes Point, boys' school, lower stream, wc).

Secondly, negative interaction between the teacher and students, in terms of giving out to or ignoring students, was seen as a characteristic of bad teachers:

Student: If they shout, you know, that shouts at you when you're after doing something wrong like. (Barrack St. School, girls' school, mixed ability class, wc).

Student: One that screams their head off at the slightest like mistake or something like that. (Harris Street, girls' school, mixed ability class, mc).

Interviewer: So what makes a really bad teacher?

Student: Boring.

Student: Strict.

Student: If they don't listen to what you're saying.

Student: Yeah if you ask a question.

Student: Or ignoring you. (Argyle Street, coed school, higher band, mxc).

Thirdly, teachers having an uninteresting style and being over-reliant on the textbook was seen as making classes boring:

Student: And I think it's bad as well a teacher like kind of teaching method is really bad, you just read from the book, just doesn't explain anything, keeps going page by page and everyone's just sitting there. (Harris Street, girls' school, mixed ability class, mc).

Not being able to maintain order in the class was also mentioned by some students:

Student: They can't control like and if you don't do your work like he just doesn't care. (Wattle St. School, boys' school, mixed ability class, mxc).

In sum, a significant proportion of students have difficulties with the pace of instruction in their class. Students see teachers who explain things clearly as contributing to their learning while teacher approachability (those they can talk to or have a laugh with) also emerges as an important characteristic of effective teaching from the student perspective.

5.3 APPROACH TO LEARNING

Students were asked about the kinds of lessons in which they learn most. The majority of second year students in the case-study schools reported that they learn best in classes where the teachers explains things really well, classes where the students like the subject a lot and they are very good at the subject (Figure 5.5). Forty per cent or more of students found classes where they could have some fun, express their opinions, work in groups and like the teacher the most helpful. Over a third of students prefer classes where there are plenty of practical activities. Classes where students copy notes from the board, where they find things out for themselves, where there is very little messing, where the teacher does most of the talking and where students are made to work hard were seen as helpful by a smaller proportion of students.

Students' opinions were analysed to assess whether their perceptions of teaching and lesson styles interrelated. These views of the learning process are outlined in Table 5.1. These dimensions must be regarded as complementary rather than competing learning styles since many students, particularly girls, mentioned a number of different factors as facilitating their learning.

Figure 5.5: Lesson characteristics (% 'very helpful')

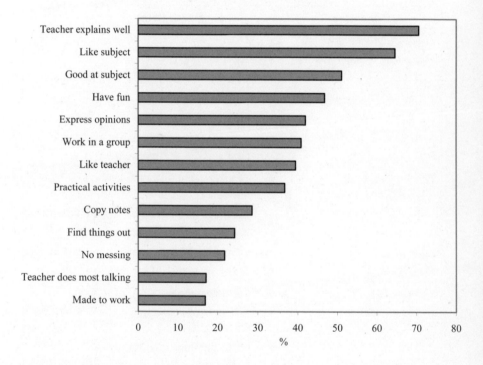

Students with lower ability levels are more likely to favour teacher-led lessons and less likely to mention intrinsic factors, such as liking the subject and the teacher. Similarly, students in lower stream classes are more likely than other ability groups to favour teacher-led lessons and less likely than those in higher stream classes to mention being good at the subject or having a good teacher. For example, the teacher doing most of the talking is more frequently seen as helpful by those in lower stream classes (73% compared with 57% in higher stream classes and 52% in mixed ability classes). This pattern across streamed classes may reflect their differing experiences of teaching and learning; research in the British context (Hallam and Ireson, 2005) has indicated that students in lower stream classes tend to have a more restricted pedagogical experience with an emphasis on repetition and didactic methods. Female students tend to mention a range of different factors as enhancing their learning while male students are more likely to favour learning as fun.

Table 5.1: Perceptions of the learning process

Dimension	Items
Having a good teacher (reliability of 0.68)	• Teachers who explain things • Teachers you can talk to • Teachers who enjoy teaching the subject
Liking the subject/teacher (reliability of 0.7)	• I like the teacher a lot • I like the subject a lot • The teachers explain things really well • I am very good at the subject
Learning as fun (reliability of 0.65)	• Teachers who relate the lesson to life outside school • Teachers who have a laugh with you • We can have some fun • I can work in a group with my friends • There are plenty of practical activities
Enquiry-based learning (reliability of 0.61)	• Teachers who praise you for good work • Teachers who encourage you to ask questions in class • I can find things out for myself • I can express my opinions in class
Teacher-led lesson (reliability of 0.55)	• Teachers who keep order in class • We are made to work hard • There is very little messing in class • The teacher does most of the talking • We copy notes from the board

Students were also asked to specify what single factor helps them learn best in class overall (see Figure 5.6). A quarter of students reported that a teacher explaining things well was the most important factor in their learning. A fifth of students mentioned teacher qualities, such as being helpful, friendly and/or kind, while over a tenth of the second years cited having a good relationship with the teacher. Having fun while learning was mentioned by almost a fifth of the students while liking or enjoying the subject was also seen as important by a significant number. Almost fifteen per cent of students mentioned having a 'good teacher' without specifying which teacher characteristics or teaching approaches worked best for them. Over a tenth of students singled out having active class-room discussion and interaction as a basis for their learning. Very few students mentioned teacher-dominated or 'traditional' classroom styles as the single most important factor in enhancing their learning.

Figure 5.6: Characteristics which help students learn best in class

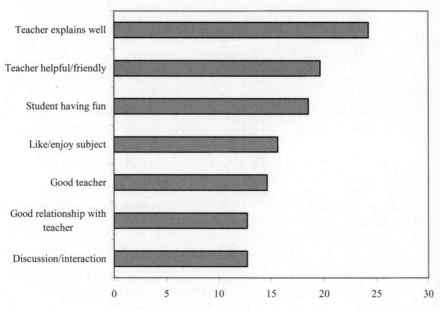

Some differences in learning preferences were apparent among groups of students. Female students were more likely to mention teachers explaining things or teacher qualities than their male counterparts. Those in mixed ability and higher stream classes were more likely to mention having a good relationship with their teacher compared with those in middle or lower stream classes.

A number of opinions were expressed by students in the group interviews as to what helps them to learn in class. Activity-based learning is the most popular among the different class groups with students mentioning discussions, teachers using different teaching styles rather than just working from the book, more practical activities in class and making the subject more interesting through different activities as helping them to learn:

> Student: It'd be better if we could have more kind of activities in class because like it can be real boring.

> Student: And you'd learn a lot more as well, we did something in French and we did a whole activity on like learning these French verbs or something and everyone knows them now even though we learnt them in class like and everyone learnt them and we didn't even try to, it was just a game really. (Argyle St. School, coed school, higher band, mxc).

> Interviewer: What do you think helps you learn in class?

> Student: Examples and getting us to do things.

> Student: Yeah, rather than just writing them all on the board.

> Student: Yeah.

> Student: And like say maybe like saying a joke about something then it'll stick in your head then.

> Student: Yeah, giving a fun method like in Geography, we have the little things that we remember stuff, like you kind of need that in other subjects as well.

> Student: Yeah.

> Student: [The teacher]'s very lively and like runs around the class and stuff so you kind of remember that.

> Student: Yeah, you remember. (Harris St. School, girls' school, mixed ability class, mc).

Linked to the idea of activity-based learning in the class, students in many of the class groups also mention that they feel that teachers explaining topics rather than just reading from the book helps them to learn better; this is unsurprising as students mentioned 'explaining things' as the most important characteristic of a good teacher in both the questionnaires and group interviews:

> Interviewer: In class are you mostly working from your book or do the teachers put notes on the board?
>
> Student: With Mr. [teacher] it's more like he explains it.
>
> Student: You don't use a book mostly.
>
> Student: He just explains it himself.
>
> Student: He just starts talking about it.
>
> Interviewer: So would you prefer that to working from a book?
>
> Three students together: Yeah.
>
> Student: A lot more interesting. (Dawes Point School, boys' school, middle stream, wc).

> Interviewer: What helps you learn in class?
>
> Student: The teacher comes in and helps you, explains.
>
> Student: Explains stuff not just giving out to us. (Hay St. School, coed School, lower stream, wc).

> Interviewer: What makes you learn best in the class, I mean like what gets you really interested?
>
> Student: If the teacher kind of explains a lot more.
>
> Student: If they explain it, it helps you like. (Wattle St. School, boys' school, mixed ability class, mxc).

Three of the class groups responded that they do not learn in class when asked what helps them to learn. Two of these class groups are lower stream classes and one is mixed ability:

> Interviewer: What helps you to learn inside the class?
>
> (Silence)

Interviewer: Like what makes the lessons really interesting?

(Silence)

Interviewer: Is there anything that makes the lesson interesting?

Three students together: No.

Student: Especially not in our work anyways. (Dixon St. School, coed school, lower stream, wc).

When the class groups are asked if they prefer working from the book or from notes written on the board, the majority of students prefer to learn from notes taken down from the board rather than directly from the text-book:

Interviewer: Would you prefer if the teachers works from the book or gives you notes from the board?

Student: Notes from the board.

Student: Notes from the board.

Interviewer: Do you think that works better?

Student: Yeah.

Student: Because if you take them down you'd know them, if you'd to look over them.

Student: Sometimes the book is not really good, bad books don't really teach you much. (Park St. School, boys' school, middle stream class, mxc).

Many of the class groups mentioned that they preferred to work in groups within class because they could exchange ideas with other students and thus found the work easier. Group work was not seen negatively by any of the students interviewed:

Interviewer: Why do you like working in groups?

Student: It's just more . . .

Student: It's, you know, nicer.

Student: More fun like.

Student: Yeah.

Student: Than just sitting there on your own and writing the whole time.

Student: Yeah, it's not as much pressure.

Student: Like in French we do loads of oral talking, it's much better than writing it all down.

Student: And say if you don't know you can like ask people or if people don't know they can ask you.

Student: Yeah.

Student: Yeah they can.

Student: Instead of sitting in a class where you can't talk at all or do anything. (Harris St. School, girls' school, mixed ability class, mc).

Interviewer: Why would you like the group work more?

Student: Because it'd be easier.

Student: And you'd have other people helping you and giving you ideas and all. (Dixon Street, coed School, lower stream, wc).

Classes in different schools had varying attitudes to whether they would ask a teacher a question in class if they did not understand something. The students in Barrack St., a predominantly working-class girls' school, said that they were sometimes afraid to ask a question in class because of the response from teachers:

Interviewer: If you didn't understand something in class would you ask the teacher?

Student: Yeah we would.

Student: The last time I did that, I nearly got freaked at.

Student: Yeah sometimes you're afraid to ask

Student: Cause she'd call you stupid, she'd go 'you're stupid'. (Barrack St. School, girls' school, mixed ability class, wc).

In contrast, students in Hay St. school, another working-class school, were the most positive about asking teachers questions in class if they did not understand something. Across all of the case-study schools, students' willingness to ask teachers to clarify issues in class depended on the individual teacher with students seeing some teachers as more approachable than others:

> Student: It depends on the teacher if you can ask questions to or not, some teachers you can keep asking questions to and they'll answer them and some teachers are just like the question you ask them, they brush it aside it and all and they don't like pay attention. (Harris Street, girls' School, mixed ability class, mc).

> Interviewer: If you didn't understand something in class would you ask the teacher?

> Student: No.

> Student: Well it depends on what class it was, some teachers you wouldn't have a problem, you'd ask them a question and they'd answer it and some teachers . . ., they just make you look stupid. (Park St. School, boys' school, higher stream class, mxc).

Only the lower stream in Dawes Point school reported that they would not ask any of their teachers questions in class if they did not understand the topic. Many students preferred to ask a classmate rather than their teachers if they did not understand something:

> Student: You would not ask the teacher, you would ask the student.

> Student: The teacher would go on about it for half and hour but your friend would just tell you how it is in about five minutes and they [the teacher] would go on for half an hour. (Belmore Street, girls' school, mixed ability class, mxc).

In general, as with their views on effective learning, students' accounts of effective lessons emphasised the teacher explaining things well as well as teacher approachability. Intrinsic interest in a subject, that is, liking the subject and being good at it, was also seen as the key to effective learning.

5.4 STUDENT ATTITUDES TO LEARNING

Students were asked about their attitudes to learning across a range of dimensions. Figure 5.7 presents the extent to which their attitudes were influenced by their peer group. Just under half of the students agreed with the statement that 'it is important for me to be seen as clever in my class'. However, over half of the students surveyed reported that they don't like people who want to show they're clever in class and around a third feel that being part of a group in school is more important than doing well. Around a third are embarrassed by praise from the teacher and a similar proportion report that they sometimes pretend they haven't studied for tests so that they won't look stupid if they do badly.

Figure 5.7: Peer effects and student attitudes to learning

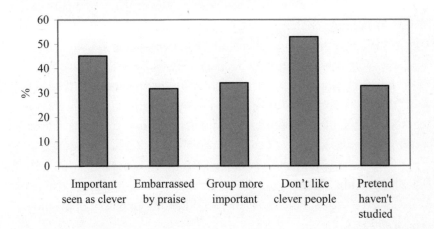

Some differences are evident between groups of students in the perceived influence of their peer group on their learning. Male students are more likely to say it is important to them to be seen as clever by their classmates, a pattern that holds within coed schools. However, they are also somewhat more likely to think that being part of the group is more important than doing well at school. On closer inspection, this pattern appears to be due to the gender distribution across schools rather than differences between girls and boys in the same school. Female students are more likely to get embarrassed if praised by teachers, a pattern which holds within coed schools (with the exception of Argyle St. school). There are no significant gender differences in not liking people to show they're clever in class and in pretending not to have studied when it comes to tests/exams. In keeping with Elwood (2003), therefore, it would appear that viewing all boys as resisting school achievement and all girls as conforming to school norms is over-simplistic; girls and boys in the case-study schools appear to be equally critical of 'show-offs' although there are some tensions in boys' perceptions between wanting to be seen as clever and wanting to be part of the group.

The relationship between attitudes to learning and prior reading/maths ability is not clear-cut; it is not simply the case that lower ability students are more resistant to achievement. What seems to make more difference than actual ability is how students define their academic performance in relation to that of their peers. Students who consider themselves as 'above average' were more likely than 'below average' students to report it is important to be seen as clever (61% compared with 40%). In contrast, below average students along with those in lower stream classes were more reliant on their peer group rather than their academic achievement for their identity. 'Below average' students were more likely to say being part of a group is more important than doing well, that they don't like people who show they're clever in class and that they pretend they haven't studied when it comes to exams. Those in lower stream classes are somewhat more likely to agree that being part of a group is more important than doing well (47% compared with 32% in top classes and 33% in mixed ability classes). Thus, it appears that some students have begun to define their social identity in partial opposition to school success.

Figure 5.8: Student attitudes to learning

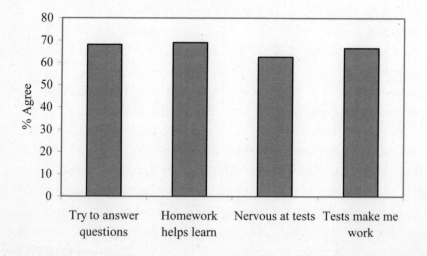

Figure 5.8 indicates that over two-thirds of second year students in the case-study schools are positive about, and invest in, certain aspects of student assessment, that is, they always try to answer questions in class, they report that doing homework helps them to learn and that tests or exams make them work. Sixty-three per cent also report they get nervous when doing tests or exams.

There is no consistent variation by prior ability in student views on assessment and learning. However, students who consider themselves above average are more likely to say that homework helps them to learn (73% compared with 55% for below average students) and that tests make them work hard (76% compared with 39%). They are also more likely to say that they always try to answer questions in class (74% compared with 51%). There is little systematic variation in responses by class type; however, those in lower stream classes are more likely to say that homework helps them learn and are somewhat more likely than those in higher stream classes to get nervous about exams. Both girls and boys report always trying to answer questions in class and are positive about the impact of homework on their learning. Female students are somewhat more likely than male students to report that tests make them work hard but also tend to get more nervous about these tests and exams.

During the group interviews in the case-study schools, student perceptions of people who study were discussed along with issues relating to homework, tests and exams. There are strong links between all aspects of students' perceptions of studying. Most class groups say that there are people in their class who study a lot, although people who study were made out to be in the minority. Those who study are generally described negatively but half of the class groups deny that these students are teased despite describing them with negative labels. Students generally think it is a good idea to study but most also say that they are not studying although they believe it is a good idea:

> Student: It's a good idea [to study] but it doesn't necessarily mean people do it. (Dawes Point School, boys' school, higher stream class, wc).

Most students said they would pretend they had not studied even when they had, and also said that it was acceptable for other students to study as long as they also do not admit that they have studied. There are two reasons for students not wanting their classmates to know that they have been studying. The first is that they are afraid they will be teased for studying or appearing to study:

> Interviewer: Just say there was an exam coming up, do you think people in your class would let on that they're studying for it or would they kind of say ah no I'm not bothered?
>
> Student: They'd say they're not bothered.
>
> Interviewer: Would they?
>
> Student: Yeah.
>
> Interviewer: Why do you think they'd say that?
>
> Student: Because they're afraid of being called a swot. (Hay Street School, coed school, higher stream class, wc).

Secondly, the students do not want others to know they are studying in case they do badly:

> Interviewer: Just say there's a test, do you think people let on that they studied for it?
>
> Student: No, they say they didn't study for it.
>
> Interviewer: Even if they have?
>
> Student: Yeah even if they have.
>
> Interviewer: And why do you think they say that?
>
> Student: So if they fail they'll be able to say I didn't study for it. (Park Street, boys' school, higher stream, mxc).

Such responses were evident across a range of schools with differing characteristics in terms of gender and social mix.

Some students in the group interviews tend to see students who study hard in the class as 'swots' who are usually antisocial and quiet:

> Student: The people who are studying won't even leave their door, they're boring.
>
> Student: Yeah they don't even go outside, that's why they study because they've no friends.

> Student: They're grand but . . . they've nothing else to do. (Lang St. School, boys' school, lower stream class, wc).

> Student: Most of them are real quiet though, they won't talk that much.

> Student: No and they wouldn't be going out at weekends. They wouldn't have enough time to do all that and go out as well. (Argyle St., coed school, higher band, mxc)

Many of the class groups admit that students who are seen to be studying hard are teased, particularly if these students show off about the good results they have obtained:

> Student: Some of them are a bit stuck up about it and they're always showing off what they get on their test but some people are ok because they don't really tell anybody what they get. (Fig Lane School, coed school, mixed ability class, mc).

Such teasing took place across a number of the schools but appeared to be somewhat less common in girls' schools. Students in Belmore St. school in particular tended to be more positive about students who study hard in second year.

5.5 HOMEWORK

The previous section indicated that the majority of second year students in the case-study schools felt that homework helped them to learn. Second year students in the case-study schools typically report spending one to two hours on homework (Figure 5.9). Female students report spending significantly more time on homework than male students (100 compared to 79 minutes), a difference which is evident within coed schools. Variation by social class is not marked but those from semi/unskilled manual backgrounds tend to spend the least amount of time on homework. Above average students spend the most time, and below average students the least time, on homework (95 compared with 60 minutes) but the relationship with prior ability is not clear-cut. Within streamed schools, students in lower stream classes tend to spend less time on homework than those in higher stream classes. Those who work part-time spend less time on homework but the difference is not statistically significant.

Students who spend longer on homework tend to be students with more positive views of school-life and their teachers but these students are also more likely to be somewhat isolated or anxious within school. Students in predominantly working-class schools (with the exception of Barrack St. girls' school) tend to spend less time on homework, a pattern that is partially related to the greater prevalence of streaming in these schools. The highest levels of homework time are found in Belmore St., a mixed intake girls' school, and Argyle St., a mixed intake coed school.

Over half of the students in the case-study schools reported that they 'get too much homework in this school'. Below average students were more likely to agree with this statement than other students though there is little variation by actual ability levels. Students in higher or middle stream classes were more likely to agree with this statement than those in lower stream classes, indicating different academic demands and teacher expectations for the different groups. There is no clear-cut relationship between complaining of too much homework and the actual amount of time spent on homework. However, students spend more time on home-work if they feel that this is a productive way of learning.

Figure 5.9: Amount of time spent on homework per weekday evening as reported by students

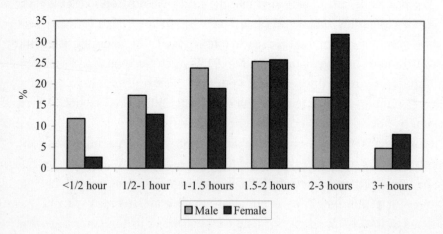

The issue of homework as a tool for learning arose in the group interviews with students in the case-study schools. The majority of the class groups do see the benefit of homework as a tool to help them learn but class groups in five of the schools (Dawson Street, Park Street, Belmore Street, Fig Lane and Dawes Point, schools with very different profiles) were split between agreeing that it helps them learn and believing that it doesn't help them to learn. Among those who say it helps them to learn, Maths homework is seen as particularly important in helping students to learn:

Interviewer: Do you think homework helps you to learn?

Student: Yeah.

Student: Yeah.

Student: In a lot of subjects it does.

Student: Especially in Maths, if he explains it.

Student: That's the only way you can learn Maths.

Student: Yeah you can't just learn Maths by reading it, you have to do it out.

Student: You have to do a load of questions. (Park St. School, boys' school, higher stream class, mxc).

Although the majority of students do see the benefit of homework, at least in theory, many students felt that a lot of their homework was rote in nature and therefore did not enhance their learning. Thus, homework was seen as a 'required' task rather than a basis for learning. This view was most commonly expressed in the three girls' schools:

Interviewer: Do you think homework helps you learn?

Student: I don't think so.

Student: Not all the time.

Student: When you're doing homework like you just kind of do it, you wouldn't really learn over it, like you just do it out quickly and then throw it to the side.

Student: Yeah.

Student: You just try and get it over and done with. (Harris St. School, girls' school, mixed ability class, mxc).

Student: And sometimes you get pointless homework

Student: Sometimes you are just opening the book and writing down whatever is in the book and it does not go in, it is just homework and we have to have it done by tomorrow. But it does not sink in.

Student: If you are writing from the book you are can be thinking about something else, you would not think about what you are writing.

Student: And I have to have this in tomorrow who cares about what it says.

Student: Just get it over and done with. (Belmore Street, girls' school, mixed ability class, mxc).

This was seen to be the case particularly if the homework load was considered heavy:

Interviewer: And does homework help you learn do you think?

Student: Yeah.

Student: But only if you have a little bit, like when you have too much homework . . . you don't be bothered, you just write anything. (Barrack Street, girls' school, mixed ability class, wc).

While students did not always feel that homework aided their learning, they felt that teachers give them homework in the belief that it helps them to learn. Again it was mainly students in the girls' schools that expressed this opinion:

Interviewer: And why do you think teachers give you homework if it doesn't help you learn?

Student: Because they might think it helps you learn.

Student: To get through the course quickly.

Student: More or less they give you homework just in case you're in school and you learn it all and then you go home and you just forget everything you've learned like if you've something to do in your homework that like to cling onto like to think about what we've done during class and stuff like that. I'd say that's why they give you homework. (Harris St. School, girls' school, mixed ability class, mc).

Students reported that teachers varied in whether they checked that homework had been done, in keeping with national survey findings from the 1990s (Smyth, 1999).

The lower stream classes emerged as a distinct group in their attitudes to homework. Most students in these classes reported that they did not get homework on a regular basis, a pattern that was seen to reflect their lower academic achievement and their unwillingness to do homework:

Student: We don't get homework.

Interviewer: Never?

Student: Just Maths, that's the odd time.

Student: Yeah.

Student: We get the chance to do Maths homework in school.

Student: In Science we just fill in the blank and they tell you all the answers.

Student: Yeah.

Interviewer: How much time would you end up spending on homework at home?

Student: Ten minutes.

Student: Five minutes

Student: I've never done homework at home.

Interviewer: Why do you think you don't get as much homework?

Student: We're no good in class.

Interviewer: Do you think that's why?

Student: Yeah.

Student: Because we don't do the homework.

Student: Because we don't do our homework.

Student: Yeah.

Student: They can give it to us all they want but it's not going to be done by tomorrow. (Dawes Point School, boys' school, lower stream class, wc).

These opinions are consistent with the views expressed by some teachers in streamed schools who reported that they tended not to give homework to the lower stream groups because they would not do it (see Chapter Three).

5.6 SUPPORT FOR LEARNING

Students were asked about the extent to which they received extra assistance, either formal or informal, with their learning. Such assistance included help from family, grinds or private tuition, assistance within school and formal learning support.

Over two-thirds of students received some help with their parents or siblings with homework or study (Figure 5.10); 14 per cent received such help frequently while 56 per cent received such help occasionally. Family help was most commonly received with Maths (57%), Irish (30%), English (10%) and French (10%). Female students are more likely than male students to report that they sometimes get help with homework. Students with lower reading/maths scores are more likely to report that they get frequent help. Similarly, those in lower stream classes are most likely, and those in higher and mixed ability classes least likely, to receive such help (29% compared with 12% and 13%).

Twelve per cent of the students surveyed had taken grinds or private tuition in the course of second year. These grinds were usually in Maths (47%), Irish (35%) and French (19%). There is no variation by gender in the take-up of grinds. Students who consider themselves below average are more likely to have taken grinds than above average students (27% compared with 11%) but the relationship with actual ability levels is not clear-cut. Students in Fig Lane school, a fee-paying school, are most likely, and those in Barrack St., Hay St. and Dawes Point, all predominantly working-class schools, least likely, to have taken grinds in second year. Thus, access to grinds appears to reflect economic resources as well as perceived 'need' of assistance.

Figure 5.10: Assistance with learning

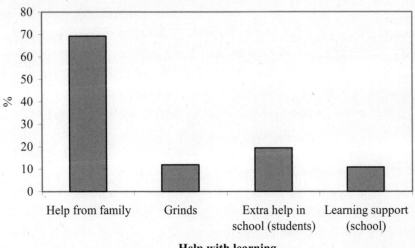

Help with learning

Students were asked about the extent to which they had received extra help within school; students interpreted this to cover informal help from individual teachers as well as formal learning support. Thirteen per cent reported receiving such help at the time of the survey (March) while 6 per cent had received help earlier in the year. Such assistance tended to be in Maths (56%), English (36%) and Irish (18%). This was most commonly on a small group (48%) or one-to-one (41%) basis. Fifty-five per cent of the students concerned found this help useful 'a lot', 29 per cent found it 'a little' useful while 16 per cent said it was 'not really' useful. Male students are more likely to have received extra help, a pattern which is due to the gender distribution across schools as only in Argyle St. did more boys than girls receive such help. Students from semi/unskilled manual and non-employed backgrounds are most likely to have received such support. Students from minority groups, those newly arrived in Ireland and those from Traveller backgrounds, are also more likely to have received extra help at school than other groups of students. Students who rate themselves as below average are more likely to have received such support than 'above average' students (34% compared with 7% in terms of help at the time of the survey) as are students with lower reading and maths scores. Those in lower stream classes are most likely, and those in mixed ability classes least likely, to have received extra help (35% for lower stream classes, 15% for higher stream classes and 12% for mixed ability classes in terms of current help). Reported receipt of extra help was found to be highest in Hay St. and Dawes Point schools, both predominantly working-class schools, and lowest in Park St. and Wattle St. schools, both boys' schools which were mixed in intake.

Of those who had not received extra help at school, a significant minority (42%) of students would have liked such help. Generally, students wanted help with Maths (45%), Irish (39%), French (18%) and Science (14%). Female students are more likely to report wanting extra help (48% compared with 35%), a difference that is evident within coed schools. A somewhat higher proportion of those from manual backgrounds would like extra help. Students of lower prior ability and those who consider themselves below average are more likely than above average students to want extra help (71% compared with 34%). Those in lower stream classes are less likely to want extra help than those in any other class types. The variation across schools in the proportion of students who would like extra help within school is not significant, suggesting that a considerable proportion of all second year students feel in need of extra help with their school work.

According to school reports, 11 per cent of students had received formal learning support, that is, sessions with a learning support or resource teacher, in the course of second year.[1] Male students are more likely to have received such help (14% compared with 8%). With the exception of Dawson St. school, male students are more likely to receive learning support than female students in the same school. Those from semi/unskilled manual and non-employed backgrounds are most likely to have received such support. Such support is targeted on students with lower reading and maths scores and is more prevalent among those who rate themselves as below average (22% compared with 7% of 'above average' students). In contrast to student reports, formal learning support is not targeted on students newly arrived in Ireland, a pattern that may be related to extra language provision not being counted as 'learning sup-

---

[1] It should be noted that data on Fig Lane were not available.

port' by schools. Students from Traveller backgrounds are more likely to have received such help (38% compared with 9%). Those in lower stream classes are most likely, and those in higher stream classes least likely, to have received extra help (49% for lower stream classes, 3% for higher stream classes and 8% for mixed ability classes). Receipt is highest in Dixon St. school (due to the use of team teaching whereby two teachers work with the same class simultaneously) and also in Hay St. and Dawes Point schools, all three predominantly working-class schools which use streaming, and lowest in Park St. and Argyle St. schools, schools which are mixed in student intake.

In sum, a considerable proportion of students across the case-study schools were receiving extra assistance with their schoolwork either on a formal or an informal basis. In spite of this pattern, a significant minority of students felt the need for extra help. It is worth noting that Maths emerges as the subject with which students receive most help in the shape of assistance from teachers, grinds and support from their family. However, students are also most likely to feel in need of extra help with Maths.

5.7 SUBJECTS IN SECOND YEAR

5.7.1 Number of subjects

Chapter Two indicated that the case-study schools differed in the timing of subject choice with some schools requiring students to select their subjects before entering the school in first year while others allowed students to sample subjects for part or all of first year before making their final decision. This meant that first year students varied considerably in the number of subjects they were taking, depending on the school they attended (see Smyth et al., 2004). By second year, students had selected their Junior Certificate subjects and so differences between schools in the number of subjects were reduced. However, some differences were still evident; students in Dawson St., Lang St. and Harris St., schools which were quite different in their socio-economic profile, tended to study thirteen subjects compared with an average of twelve in the remainder of the schools.

Differences were more evident within rather than between schools in the number of subjects taken. Students in receipt of formal learning support, those with lower reading scores and students from Traveller backgrounds tend to take slightly fewer subjects than other students. This reflects the fact that, in some cases, students are withdrawn from certain subject classes for learning assistance and/or students experiencing learning difficulties are sometimes allowed to drop certain subjects. Students whose parents come from outside Ireland also tend to take slightly fewer subjects, mainly because they have an exemption from studying Irish (see below). Within streamed schools, students in the higher stream classes tend to take slightly more subjects than those in the lower streams (an average of 12.6 compared with 11.9).

One of the differences in subject workload arises in relation to Irish. Across the case-study schools, 8 per cent of students do not take the subject. This is more common among students in lower stream classes; 22 per cent do not study Irish compared with 10 per cent of those in the higher stream. It is also more common among students receiving formal learning support (35%), students whose parents come from outside Ireland (42%), students from the Traveller community (23%) and students with lower ability levels (17% of those in the lowest reading quintile). The proportion of students not studying Irish varies considerably across the case-study schools, from none of those in Lang St. to a third in Barrack St. and 45 per cent in Hay St., reflecting the prevalence of learning difficulties and the ethnic mix within the schools.

In spite of potential concerns about 'curriculum overload', there is no evidence that taking more subjects on average is associated with more negative student experiences. Those taking more subjects do not differ from other students in their perception of schoolwork in second year, the time spent on homework and their attitudes to school. Students who report taking fewer subjects are more likely to report having trouble keeping up with their schoolwork, but this pattern reflects their underlying learning difficulties rather than the workload per se.

5.7.2 Subject choice

In the second year survey, students were asked about two aspects of subject choice: the extent to which they would have liked to take other subjects than the ones they were currently taking and whether they regretted taking any of their current subjects. Subject choice at junior cycle is likely to have important consequences for subject take-up at senior cycle and even on transition to higher education (Millar and Kelly, 1999; Smyth and Hannan, 2002).

Over half (58%) of second year students in the case-study schools reported that there are subjects they would like to have taken but couldn't or didn't in their school because these subjects were not available or because they were not given access to them. The subjects most commonly mentioned were subjects with a more practical component (namely, Materials Technology (Wood) (24%), Metalwork (16%), Home Economics (16%), Computer Studies (14%) and Art (14%)) along with Spanish (17%). Over half (57%) of the students reported they could not take the subject in question because it was not provided in their school, 13 per cent said they weren't allowed to take it by the school, 12 per cent said that it clashed on the timetable with another subject, 5 per cent reported that too many students wanted to take it while 2 per cent reported that not enough students wanted to take it. The proportion of students who report restricted subject choice does not vary across class type. However, the reasons for not being able to take the subject do vary; not being allowed to take the subject by the school was more commonly reported by those in lower and middle stream classes (31% and 21%) than those in higher stream or mixed ability classes (10%). Restricted subject choice is somewhat more frequently reported in Barrack St. and Park St. schools, both schools where students were required to pick their subjects before entry. However, it is not systematically related to whether or not the school had a 'taster' programme where students tried out different subjects before choosing them. The absence of such a pattern is most likely related to the fact that the central issues were the lack of provision of specific subjects in the school and the restricted access to certain subjects among streamed classes rather than to the way in which subject choice in the school was framed.

A similar proportion (59%) of second year students report that there are subjects they are now taking that they would prefer not to have taken. Students interpreted this to cover all subjects (including compulsory subjects) not just subjects over which they had a choice. The most frequently mentioned subjects were French (18%), Business Studies (17%), Irish (15%), Science (14%), German (11%) and History (10%). It is interesting to note that very few (6%) of students mentioned not wanting to have taken Maths, perhaps reflecting the fact that they see it as a useful subject (see below). Reasons for their preferences included not liking the subject (e.g. finding it boring) (57%), finding the subject hard (46%), not needing the subject (20%), not liking the teacher (17%), not being good at the subject (14%) and having too much to learn (5%). 'Below average' students were more likely than above average students to specify subjects they would prefer not to take (80% compared with 52%). Variation across schools is not clear-cut; students in Barrack St. and Harris St. schools, girls' schools with contrasting intakes in socio-economic terms, were most likely, and those in Fig Lane and Belmore St. schools least likely, to specify subjects. The lack of variation between 'taster' and other schools in the proportion of students who regretted taking certain subjects is most likely due to the fact that students interpreted this to include subjects, such as Irish, which they were required to take rather than just the subjects they selected themselves.

Dissatisfaction with subject choice is associated with more general orientation to school life among second year students. Students who reported restricted subject choice or who regretted taking certain subjects had significantly more negative attitudes to school and to their teachers than other groups of students. This pattern was evident even controlling for whether students were in a streamed school or not. Thus, being dissatisfied with the package of subjects available to them may alienate students from being engaged in schoolwork in the longer term.

5.7.3 Attitudes to specific subjects

The previous section considered student attitudes to the package of subjects they are taking. This section explores student perceptions of specific subject areas in second year across a range of dimensions.

Students were asked to report the two subjects they liked most in second year. Because of differences in the take-up rates of the various subjects, the figures are based on those taking the relevant subjects. The most frequently mentioned subjects comprised subjects with a practical orientation: Art, the technological subjects, Home Economics, Music and Physical Education with none of the 'core' academic subjects (such English, Maths and foreign languages) mentioned by more than a fifth of the cohort (Figure 5.11).

Female students were more likely than male students to name English, French and Art as their favourite subjects while they were less likely than male students to name Materials Technology (Wood), Technology or PE. Students with lower reading scores and those who considered themselves below average are more likely to name Art or Materials Technology (Wood) as their favourite subject. Lower stream classes are more likely than higher stream classes to name Materials Technology (Wood) or Computer Studies[2] as their favourite subject.

Figure 5.11: Favourite subjects in second year

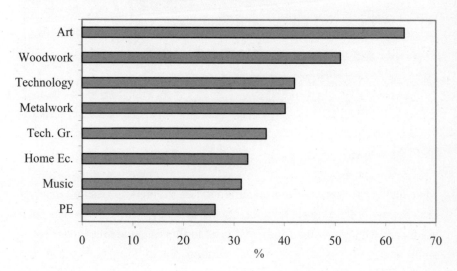

---

[2] Computer Studies is not a recognised examination subject but was provided at junior cycle level in two-thirds of schools in 2002/3 (Department of Education and Science Statistical Report 2002/3).

Students were also asked to report the two subjects they liked least in second year. The most frequently mentioned subject was Irish (mentioned by 32 per cent of those taking the subject), followed by foreign languages, Maths, Business Studies, Science, Geography and History (Figure 5.12). Female students are more likely than male students to name History or Science as their least favourite subject. Above average students are somewhat more likely to name Irish or CSPE as their least favourite subject while below average students are more likely to name French. There is little systematic variation in least favourite subject across class types, although students in the higher stream are somewhat more likely to mention Geography than those in middle or lower stream classes.

Figure 5.12: Subjects like least in second year

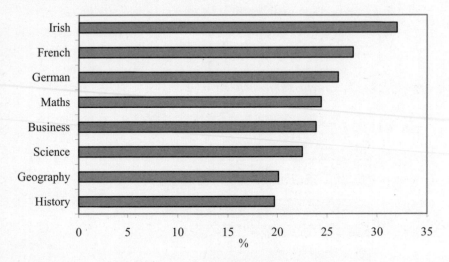

Students were asked to rate a specified list of subjects across a number of dimensions, including difficulty, interest and usefulness. Irish was seen as difficult by more than half of the second year students in the case-study schools. Almost half of the students found French, Science and Maths difficult (Figure 5.13). On the other hand, fewer than ten per cent of students found PE and Computer Studies difficult. Female students are somewhat more likely to find Science, History, Geography and German difficult than male students and less likely to find English, French, Art and Home Economics difficult. As would be expected, students who consider themselves below average are more likely to find the specified subjects difficult than 'above average' students. However, when actual ability levels are considered, students with higher reading scores tend to find Maths and Irish difficult, reflecting the level at which they are studying the subject, while lower ability students find French difficult. Students in higher stream classes are somewhat more likely to find English, History, Geography and Irish difficult than those in lower stream classes, most likely reflecting academic demands and pace of instruction in these classes. There is considerable variation across schools in the perceived difficulty of certain subjects, reflecting both particular teachers as well as differences in student intake into the school.

Figure 5.13: Subject difficulty

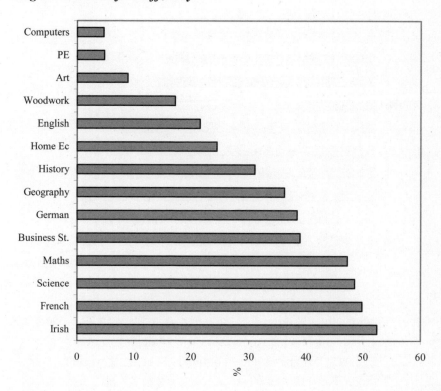

Second year students in the case-study schools are more likely to see subjects with a practical orientation (e.g. Art, Materials Technology (Wood), Computers, PE, Home Economics) as interesting than they are the more traditional 'academic' subjects. While a considerable proportion of students found Science difficult (see above), the majority of students found it interesting (Figure 5.14). Over half of students found History, English, Geography, Business Studies and Maths interesting. Levels of interest in languages were somewhat lower than for other subjects; just under half of the second year students in the case-study schools found French and German interesting while just over a third found Irish interesting.

Figure 5.14: Subjects perceived as interesting

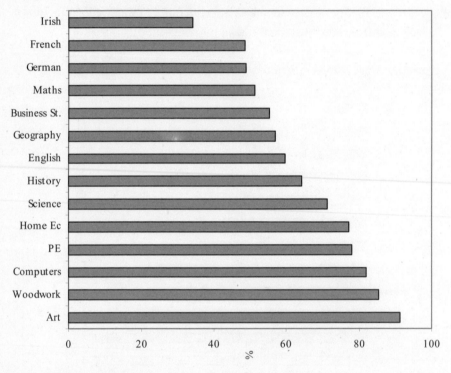

Some variation among groups of students is evident in the extent to which they find subjects interesting. Female students are more likely to find the languages, Art and Home Economics interesting while male students are more likely to find History, Computers, PE and, to some extent, Science interesting. Students with lower reading scores express less interest in French and more interest in Maths and Irish than those with higher test scores. There is also variation across classes in levels of student interest in the various subjects. Students in lower stream classes are more likely to find Maths, English, Geography, Irish and Materials Technology (Wood) interesting than those in higher stream or mixed ability classes. Those in higher stream classes are somewhat more likely to find History, Geography, French and Computers interesting than those in lower stream classes. As with perceived difficulty in particular subjects, there is some variation across schools in the levels of student interest.

In general, second year students tend to see the subjects they take as useful. The vast majority saw Maths, Home Economics, Woodwork, Business Studies and Computers as useful (Figure 5.15). The subjects seen as least useful by students were History (50%) and Irish (46%). Male students are more likely than female students to report that History, Materials Technology (Wood) and PE are useful while female students are more likely to see Home Economics, French and German as useful. Students from a higher professional or farming background are more likely to see foreign languages as useful than those from semi/unskilled manual backgrounds. Students with lower reading scores are less likely to see foreign languages and Science as useful. Students in lower stream classes are more likely to see English as useful than those in higher stream or mixed ability classes and are somewhat more likely to see Geography and Irish as useful. However, they are less likely to see French as useful (44% compared with 65% in higher stream and 70% in mixed ability classes). As with other attitudes to subjects, there is some variation by school in the perceived utility of subjects.

Overall, second year students tended to feel that about the right amount of time was devoted to the specified subjects (Figure 5.16). The exceptions were Computer Studies and Physical Education where over half of the students surveyed felt that too little time was devoted to these subjects. A third of students felt that too much time was allocated to Irish while over a quarter considered too much time was given to French and German. In contrast, over a quarter wanted more time spent on Art while a third wanted more time spent on Materials Technology (Wood). Students of lower academic ability levels tend to think that too much time is spent on some of the more academic subjects, such as Science, History and Geography, in contrast to more academically able students who feel too little time is spent on these subjects.

Figure 5.15: Subjects useful

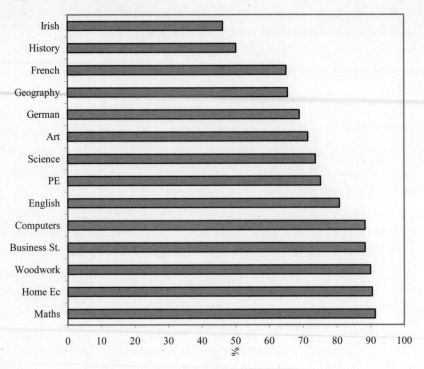

Figure 5.16: Time allocated to subjects

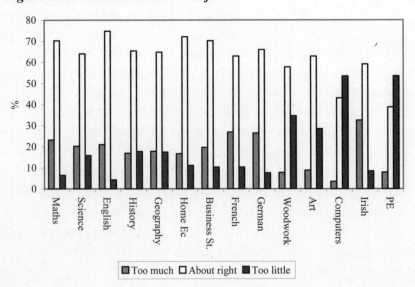

5.8 FUTURE ASPIRATIONS: EDUCATION, OCCUPATION AND FAMILY

The previous sections of this chapter have sought to depict the learning experiences of second year students. This section looks at the extent to which second year students are oriented to the future in terms of thinking about the Junior Certificate examination along with their longer term educational and career aspirations.

5.8.1 The Junior Certificate examination

Across all class groups in the case-study schools, students reported that their teachers had begun to talk about the Junior Certificate exams at this stage in second year:

> They mention it every single class . . . you have to do this for the Junior Cert and you have to do that and all and this won't be good enough for Junior Cert. (Wattle St. School, boys' School, mixed ability class, mxc).

Classes are almost evenly divided between whether they think that second year is about the right time to be thinking about the Junior Certificate and those who think it is too early. Students in streamed schools were more likely to say they felt it was to early to focus on the Junior Certificate exam:

> Interviewer: Is it too early to think about Junior Cert in your second year or not?

> Student: No I don't think it's too early because it flies by, just feels like coming into the school yesterday and stuff, so it will happen in no time, so yeah I suppose they have to keep reminding us and teaching . . . prepared really. (Fig Lane School, coed School, mixed ability, mc).

> Student: You should start thinking about the Junior Cert in third year really.

> Student: Putting pressure on you this time next year, a few weeks before, about from January they should start putting pressure on you, not the year before. That'd wreck your head. (Lang St. School, boys' school, higher stream, wc).

Even in one of the more academically oriented schools, a girls' school serving a middle-class intake, the Junior Certificate exam was seen as remote in the time horizon:

> Student: But next year we'll actually have to pay attention.
>
> Student: This year it was just like . . .
>
> Student: Next year we have to actually pay attention as well.
>
> Student: That's next year.
>
> Student: Yeah, that's next year, we can worry about it then.
>
> Student: It's a long way away. (Harris Street, girls' school, mixed ability class, mc).

Only three of the class groups mention that they are thinking about the Junior Certificate at this stage in second year, focusing on the advantage of studying in second year as a preparation for third year:

> Student: Well I would like to start study now because you have to study for all three years next year then so you're easier just to start studying now than like, only if you had a small idea of it and then next year you'll know what you're talking about. (Argyle Street, coed school, higher band, mxc).

Although students were not focusing on the Junior Certificate exam in second year, the majority of class groups said they considered the exam to be important. The class groups in Harris Street are unique in stressing that how they do in the Junior Certificate is particularly important to their parents:

> Interviewer: Do you think it matters how well you do in your Junior Cert?
>
> Student: Yeah.
>
> Student: For parents it matters.
>
> Student: To my parents it really matters but like I don't really mind. I just don't wanna fail.
>
> Student: Like I'll study really hard for my Leaving but like the Junior Cert. I don't think it's that important. (Harris Street, girls' school, mixed ability class, mc).

However, many students qualified their remarks on the importance of the Junior Certificate exam, mentioning that it was not as important as the Leaving Certificate exam:

> Interviewer: Do you think Junior Cert exams are important?
>
> Student: No, because it's only a practice for the Leaving Cert.
>
> Student: Yeah but if you do bad you can't do the Leaving.
>
> Student: Yeah, they're important but they're not as important as the Leaving Cert, they are important though. (Fig Lane, coed school, mixed ability class, mc).

> Interviewer: So you think it doesn't really matter [how you do in the Junior Cert]?
>
> Student: No.
>
> Student: No.
>
> Student: Not that much.
>
> Student: You'd still want to study for it though.
>
> Student: It's a big exam, but it's not the Leaving Cert. (Park Street, boys' school, higher stream, mxc).

Six of the class groups, mainly mixed ability classes, already felt that there was a certain amount of pressure on them in relation to sitting their Junior Certificate:

> Interviewer: What kind of things do they [teachers] say about the Junior Cert?
>
> Student: Study hard.
>
> Student: And you have to know certain things for your Junior Cert.
>
> Student: And everything is associated with the Junior Cert.
>
> Student: And everything is about that.
>
> Student: And everything we do is not going to be on the Junior Cert.
>
> Student: And they make out it is.
>
> Student: And they keep on saying to work harder and do your work.
>
> Interviewer: So do you feel that you are under pressure?

Student: Yeah. (Belmore St. School, girls' school, mixed ability class, mxc).

The majority of the class groups think that the Junior Certificate will be 'hard'. Class groups in Belmore Street, Harris Street and Barrack Street (all mixed ability girls' schools) are most likely to feel that the Junior Certificate will be difficult, although views differed within as well as between classes:

Interviewer: Do you think the Junior Cert will be hard?

Student: Yeah.

Student: Yeah if you don't know your second year work how will you do your tests, if you don't understand something, especially. (Barrack St. School, girls' school, mixed ability class, wc).

Interviewer: What do you think the Junior Cert will be like?

Student: Hard.

Student: Hard.

Student: But then it seems to be getting easier every year so you don't know.

Student: It will be kind of hard. (Harris Street, girls' school, mixed ability class, mc).

Interviewer: What do you think it's going to be like yourselves?

Student: Stressful and I am worried that I would not pass it and like you know.

Student: I would not mind that much, it is only a test, like if you do well in the Junior Cert you can do well in the Leaving Cert.

Student: It does not bother me.

Student: And they [teachers] have made it such a big deal and now everyone has got used to it.

Student: You know everyone says you'll do well, but what if I don't do well?

Student: You are being pressurised. (Belmore Street, girls' school, mixed ability class, mxc).

However, some class groups reported that they felt that the exam would be 'fairly easy' (Hay St. school, middle stream, wc).

A number of students felt that the 'mock' exams before the Junior Certificate would actually be harder than the Junior Certificate itself:

> Student: I'm not like that worried about it because my sister said it's not as bad as like they make it out. It's more your Leaving Cert you get stressed about I think.

> Student: Yeah, my friend did it last year, she's in this school as well and she said the mocks were harder definitely than the Junior Cert. It wasn't as hard as she'd thought it would be. (Harris Street, girls' school, mixed ability class, mc).

> Interviewer: What do you think the Junior Cert will be like?

> Student: I heard the mocks are harder than the actual Junior Cert itself. (Park Street, boys' school, middle stream, mxc).

In general, students in mixed ability and higher stream classes were more likely to talk about the Junior Certificate examination. Those in the lower streams did not raise many issues surrounding the Junior Certificate other than the fact that their teachers have started talking about it.

5.8.2 Subject levels within the Junior Certificate

Students were asked about the level at which they expected to take Irish, English and Maths for the Junior Certificate exam. For Irish, students are almost equally divided between higher and ordinary level with a tenth expecting to take foundation level (Figure 5.17). Two-thirds of students expect to take English at higher level while over half expect to take Maths at higher level. Two per cent of students are taking all three subjects at foundation level while 3 per cent are taking two subjects at foundation level. Almost a third (32%) of students are taking all three subjects at higher level.

Figure 5.17: Levels expect to take for Junior Certificate exam

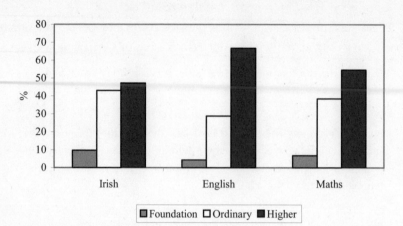

Female students are more likely to say they will take Irish and English at higher level and less likely to take foundation level; the pattern is similar for Maths but the gender differences are less marked. In general, gender differences for Irish and English are found within coed schools (although the differences in Dixon St. school are not very marked); in contrast, gender differences within schools are not significant for Maths. Those from non-manual and farming backgrounds are more likely to take Irish, English and Maths at higher level and less likely to take foundation level in these subjects. As might be expected, below average students are more likely to say they will take Irish, English and Maths at foundation level and less likely to say they will take these subjects at higher level.

In keeping with previous research (Hannan et al., 1983; Smyth, 1999), class allocation is found to be predictive of the level at which students study Junior Certificate subjects. Those in lower stream classes are more likely to intend to take Irish, English and Maths at foundation level in the Junior Cert than those in other class groups (Figure 5.18).

Figure 5.18: Proportion taking foundation level by class allocation

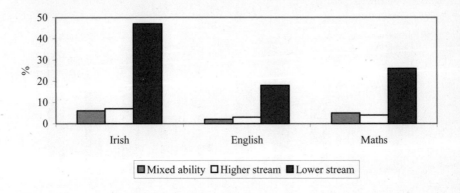

As might be expected, students with lower reading and maths scores are more likely to take foundation or ordinary level while those with higher assessed ability levels are more likely to take higher level across the three subjects. The considerable variation between schools found in the levels taken by students thus reflects differences in the ability levels of their student intake. However, a 'school effect' is evident over and above the ability profile of the school.[3] Looking at students who were in the lowest fifth on the computation test administered in first year, 69 per cent of these students in Hay St., a predominantly working-class school, expected to take foundation level but almost half (47%) of students in the same ability group in Fig Lane, a fee-paying school, expected to take higher level Maths. Similarly, schools vary in the proportion of students taking higher level English among the second lowest group in reading scores (see Figure 5.19), with very low proportions taking higher level in Dixon St., Hay St. and Wattle St. schools. This is partly but not wholly related to the social class mix of the school but school policy regarding access to higher level, teacher encouragement and the expectational climate of the school appear to play a part (see Smyth and Hannan, 2002 on take-up of higher level Maths at Leaving Certificate level).

---

[3] Argyle Street and Harris Street are not included in these analyses as they became involved in the study in the second year.

Figure 5.19: Proportion taking higher level English among second lowest reading group

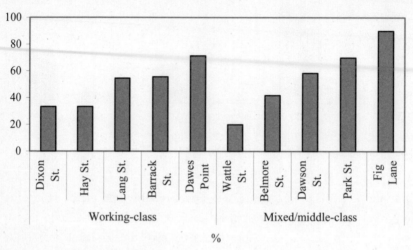

5.8.3 Educational aspirations

Students were also asked about the highest qualification they expect to receive overall; the majority (70%) expect to go on to third-level education (49% at degree level, 22% at certificate/diploma level), 23 per cent expect to reach Leaving Certificate while 7 per cent expect to terminate their education at Junior Certificate level. Female students have higher aspirations than their male counterparts; 59 per cent expect to reach degree level compared with 39 per cent of male students (Figure 5.20). These gender differences are apparent within coed schools, that is, female students tend to have higher aspirations than male students in the same school context. As might be expected given existing attainment patterns, educational aspirations are strongly differentiated by social class background; 63 per cent of those from higher professional backgrounds expect to reach degree level compared with 29 per cent of those from semi/unskilled manual backgrounds. Students who have lower reading and maths scores have lower aspirations as do students who consider themselves 'below average' (24% expect to finish at Junior Certificate level compared with 4% of 'above average' students). Lower educational aspirations are also found among those in lower stream classes; 29 per cent expect to leave at Junior Certificate level compared with 6 per cent of those in higher stream classes and 4 per cent of those in mixed abil-ity classes. Educational aspirations tend to be lower in working-class and streamed schools overall; they are highest in Fig Lane school, a fee-paying school, and lowest in Hay St. school, a school serving a predominantly working-class population. Some of the student groups in the interviews also spoke of a desire to leave school early. Students in the lower stream classes were more likely to say they would like to leave school before they attained their Leaving Certificate, a pattern that was strongest in Dixon Street, a coeducational school with designated disadvantaged status. The lower educational aspirations among students in lower streams must be seen in the context of the disaffection from, and disengagement with, school life expressed by these students (see Chapter Four).

Figure 5.20: Educational aspirations by gender

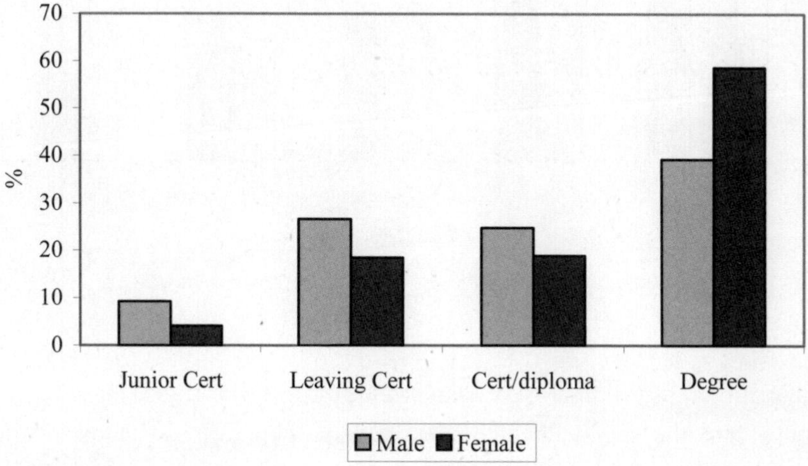

5.8.4 Career aspirations

Second year students were asked about their occupational aspirations in terms of the job they 'would aspire to' and the job they 'would settle for'. Students in the case-study schools were found to have relatively high aspirations with the majority aiming towards professional occupa-tions. When students specified jobs they 'would settle for', aspirations were somewhat more modest with a higher proportion mentioning manual occupations than had done so initially. Clear gender differences were evident in the aspirations of second year students (see Figure 5.21). Female students were less likely than their male counterparts to mention higher professional or manual occupations and more likely to aspire to lower professional occupations (which include many traditionally female jobs such as nursing and teaching). The single most commonly mentioned jobs were 'sportsmen and related workers' (12%) and carpenters/joiners (10%) for boys, and teachers (17%), hairdressers (13%) and 'actors, entertainers and musicians' (11%) for girls.

Figure 5.21: Occupational aspirations of students

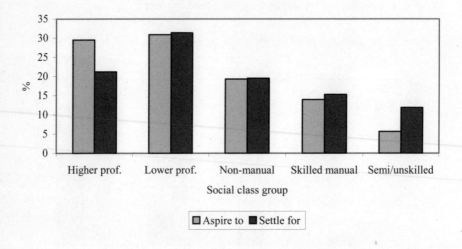

Occupational aspirations were also strongly related to social class background and the ability level of the student. Four-fifths of those from higher professional backgrounds aspired to such jobs themselves compared with forty per cent of those from semi/unskilled manual backgrounds. Similarly, almost a third of those from semi/unskilled manual backgrounds aspired to manual jobs compared with only seven per cent of those from higher professional backgrounds. Occupational aspirations are significantly related to prior ability levels in reading and maths; 15 per cent of those in the lowest fifth at reading aspire to higher professional jobs compared with half of those in the top fifth. Similarly, students who rated themselves as 'above average' in their year group were significantly more likely to aspire to higher professional jobs; 48 per cent aspired to such jobs compared with 8 per cent of those who rated themselves as below average in terms of their schoolwork.

Figure 5.22: Occupational aspirations by gender

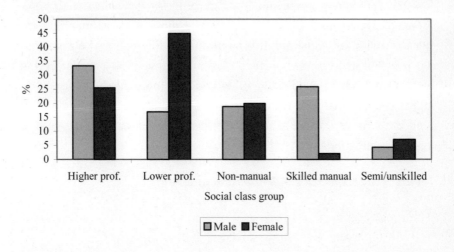

As well as being asked about their occupational aspirations, students were asked about the possible working arrangements they would have if they were married and had a family. The most commonly selected option was that the man would work full-time while the female partner would work part-time outside the home; this option was selected by more female than male students (58% compared with 38%). Over a quarter of male and female students selected the dual career option whereby both partners would work full-time outside the home (Figure 5.23). A minority of students selected a 'traditional' division of labour, a pattern which was more common among male than female students (17% compared with 8%). On the other hand, male students were also more likely to select less traditional options.

Among male students, above average students and those with higher educational aspirations are somewhat more likely to pick traditional arrangements (but the difference is not marked). Among female students, above average students are somewhat more likely to mention the dual career option and less likely to select traditional arrangements while those with the lowest reading scores are more likely to opt for a traditional division of labour. Students (both male and female) whose mothers do not work outside the home are more likely to favour the traditional option. The anticipated gender division of labour is also related to students' occupational aspirations. Among female students, those who mention the dual career arrangement are more likely than other students to aspire to higher professional careers while those who mention a traditional division of labour are disproportionately likely to aspire to a manual job. The pattern among male students is less clear-cut; those who mention a traditional division of labour are more likely to aspire to higher professional jobs than other groups of students while a relatively high proportion of those who mention the dual career option aspire to manual occupations.

Figure 5.23: Expected gender division of labour

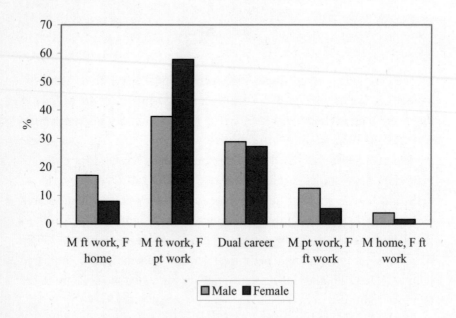

5.9 CONCLUSIONS

Two groups of students were evident among second years in the case-study schools: those for whom second year involved an intensification of their academic effort and those who were drifting, or even actively disengaging, from school. At this stage, female students, those from middle-class backgrounds, those with higher prior ability levels and those in mixed ability or higher stream classes were becoming more involved in their schoolwork while male students, those from working-class backgrounds, those with lower ability levels and those in lower stream classes were more likely to be disengaging from school life.

In terms of teaching and learning, students emphasised the importance of clarity of explanation, teacher approachability and intrinsic interest in the subject as key factors in enhancing their learning. As in first year, students were most positive about the subjects with a more practical orientation while many found the more 'academic' subjects difficult.

Although some students were becoming increasingly engaged in their schoolwork, few viewed their learning in the context of the Junior Certificate exam. However, students tended to see doing well in the exam as important. The majority of students in the case-study schools are found to have relatively high educational and career aspirations, although clear differences are already evident in terms of gender, social class background and (perceived and actual) academic ability levels.

Chapter Six

MOVING FROM FIRST TO SECOND YEAR

The longitudinal nature of this study means that we can explore changes in individual students in ten of the case-study schools over the course of first and second year. The *Moving Up* study had indicated some changes in student attitudes to school over the course of first year. Following students into their second year of the junior cycle means that we can assess whether such changes were merely short-term or are cumulative over time. The first section considers changes in student attitudes to school, in their self-image and in their attitudes to specific subject areas between first and second year; the extent to which changes may differ between groups of students is also explored. The second section assesses the impact of student academic ability and experiences of school life in first year on how they fare in second year.

6.1 CHANGES IN STUDENT ATTITUDES BETWEEN FIRST AND SECOND YEAR

6.1.1 Changes in attitudes to school and teachers

This section considers changes in student attitudes to school life over three time-points: September of first year, May of first year and March of second year. Analyses explore whether significant changes have taken place in student attitudes over the period and which groups of students have experienced such changes. Table 6.1 shows changes in attitudes to school and teachers, interaction with teachers, misbehaviour, being bullied and feeling isolated over time. The final column indicates whether these trends are statistically significant and their relative size in terms of

standard deviations.[1] Attitudes to school and to teachers are found to become less positive as students move through the junior cycle. The quality
of interaction between teachers and students changes with less emphasis
on praise and reinforcement and a greater prevalence of being 'given out
to'. Student self-reported misbehaviour increases over time but actual
rates of bullying are stable. Students are no more likely to feel isolated in
second year than in first year. The remainder of this section discusses
these changes in greater detail.

Table 6.1: Changes in overall attitudes to school life

	First Year (Sept.)	First Year (May)	Second Year	Changes between First and Second Year
Attitudes to school	2.99	2.74	2.54	Decline (p<.001; -0.3 SD)
Attitudes to teachers	3.14	2.93	2.81	Decline (p<.001; -0.2 SD)
Positive teacher-student interaction	2.50	2.56	2.42	Decline (p<.001; -0.2 SD)
Negative teacher-student interaction	1.76	1.92	2.03	Increase (p<.01; +0.1 SD))
Misbehaviour	n.a.	1.97	2.11	Increase (p<.001; +0.2 SD)
Bullying	1.17	1.27	1.24	No change
Feeling isolated	1.72	1.68	1.69	No change

Note: This table and the following tables/figures relate to the ten case-study schools included in both the first and second year studies.

Student attitudes to school are found to have become significantly less
positive over the course of first year with a further 'dip' taking place during
second year (see Table 6.1). This is consistent with other longitudinal studies which indicate that students become less engaged in school and enjoy

---

[1] In a normal distribution, 68 per cent of the sample will fall within one standard deviation
of the mean.

their schoolwork less as they move through the system (see, for example, Harland et al., 2002). Figure 6.1 indicates the patterns for each item included in the measure 'liking school'. It is clear that students have become less positive across all aspects of their attitudes to school with the greatest decline taking place in the proportion who report being excited about school, looking forward to school and finding schoolwork interesting. The proportion of students who disagree with the statement 'I find schoolwork in this school really interesting' increases from a fifth of students at the beginning of first year to almost half of students towards the end of second year.

Figure 6.1: Changes in attitudes to school

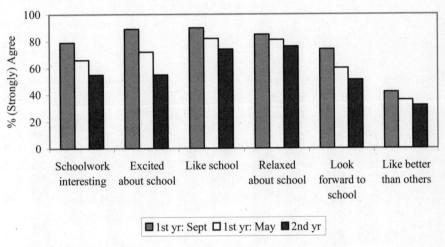

The decline in liking school is evident across all ability levels. However, the trends differ somewhat by other student characteristics. Within co-educational schools, male students report a greater decline in attitudes to school than their female counterparts. The greatest declines are found in mixed ability and lower stream classes. Declines in the proportion with positive attitudes to school are greatest in the lower stream classes in three of the streamed schools (Park St., Hay St. and Dawes Point). However, the pattern is different in the other streamed schools; within Lang St. school, the greatest decline is found in the middle stream class while the decline is greatest for the higher stream class in Dixon St.

As with attitudes to school, attitudes to teachers are found to become less positive over the course of first year with a further decline during the second year of the junior cycle (see Table 6.1), a pattern which is evident across all levels of prior ability. Two of the items, finding most teachers friendly and feeling that teachers would help them with schoolwork problems, become less positive during first year but do not change further on the transition to second year. However, the proportion of students who report liking most of their teachers, who feel they could talk to teachers about a problem and who think there is a good working atmosphere in their class declines during both first and second year. As with attitudes to school, greater declines are evident among male students in coed schools than among their female counterparts. The pattern of change varies across streamed classes but differently in the different school contexts.

Figure 6.2: Changes in attitudes to teachers

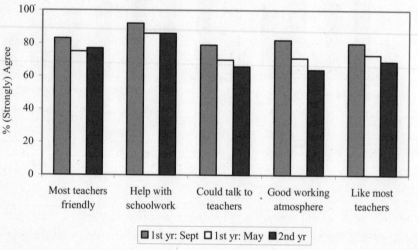

The prevalence of positive teacher-student interaction in the case-study schools does not change significantly over the course of first year; however, it does decline between first and second year, indicating that teachers' approaches may change after an initial 'honeymoon' period of positive reinforcement of students. This pattern is consistent with student accounts of teachers making greater allowances for first year students (see

Chapter Four). Changes are evident across all dimensions of the measure with a decline in the number of students who report teachers praising their work along with a decline in interaction in the class context (students being asked or asking questions). There is little systematic variation in these trends across groups of students with no significant differences by gender, prior academic ability or ability group (stream).

Figure 6.3: Changes in positive teacher-student interaction

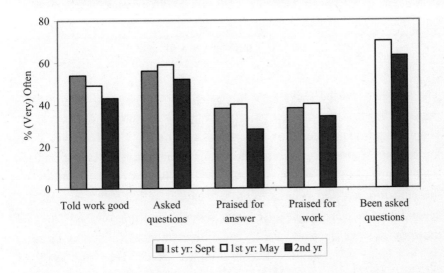

The prevalence of negative teacher-student interaction, that is, students being 'given out to' by teachers, increases considerably over the course of first year with a further increase between first and second year, especially in the number who report being given out to for misbehaviour. Within two of the coed schools (Dixon St. and Fig Lane), male students report a greater increase in negative interaction than female students but no such gender differences were evident within Dawson St. school. The pattern by ability group varied across schools and there is some evidence that students with the lowest reading scores experience the greatest increase in negative interaction with their teachers.

Figure 6.4: Changes in negative teacher-student interaction

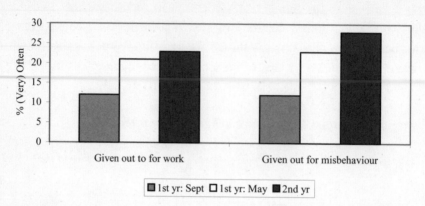

The student-reported prevalence of misbehaviour increased significantly between the first and second year of the junior cycle (see Table 6.1), in keeping with the perceptions of teachers outlined in Chapter Two. With the exception of absence from school, all forms of misbehaviour and re-lated punishment increased over the period (Figure 6.5). In particular, messing in class had become quite a frequent activity with half of the second year students in the case-study schools reporting messing three or more times since the start of the year. The incidence of skipping classes, or 'mitching', also increased from first to second year. Within coed schools, male students reported an increased level of misbehaviour com-pared with female students. Students in streamed schools reported less of an increase in misbehaviour than those in mixed ability schools. Misbe-haviour is found to increase across all academic ability levels.

Figure 6.5: Changes in student misbehaviour

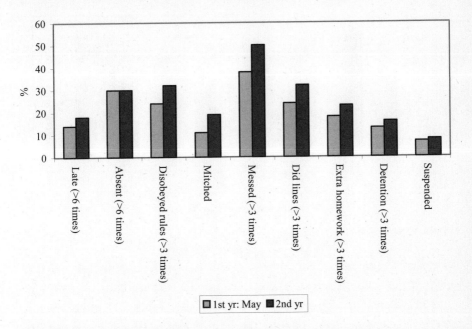

Another aspect of student misbehaviour, the prevalence of bullying, is considered in Figure 6.6. The prevalence of bullying was found to increase over the course of first year but stabilised thereafter (see Table 6.1). There was some variation across different forms of bullying; being physically pushed around seemed to be somewhat less frequent in second year than in first year while being jeered or mocked by other students increased in prevalence. There was little systematic variation by gender or academic ability in the trends between first and second year. Some schools, particularly Hay St., Lang St. and Park St., evidenced a decline in bullying levels. Within three of the streamed schools, Lang St., Park St. and Dawes Point, a decline in bullying was more marked in the lower stream class than in other class groups.

Figure 6.6: Experience of being bullied over time

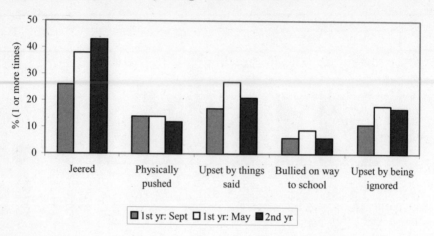

Figure 6.7 indicates trends in the extent to which students felt isolated within the school context. There were no significant trends over time in the prevalence of such feelings of isolation (see Table 6.1), either overall or by gender, academic ability and ability group. However, there were changes in respect of some items. By the end of first year, students appear to have become more socially integrated into school life with fewer reporting that they do not have many friends in the school. Encouragingly, students are somewhat less likely to be afraid of making a fool of themselves in class and are less likely to be afraid of telling a teacher if they don't understand something than they were in first year.

6.1.2 Changes in student self-image

Trends in four aspects of student self-image were analysed: academic self-rating (students' view of their own abilities), students' assessments of whether they were good at sports, body-image (students' assessment of their own appearance) and self-reported popularity with classmates. Table 6.2 indicates that students become less positive over time about their capacity to cope with school-work and about their sporting abilities. They are likely to report being less popular with their classmates but no overall changes are evident in their body-image. The decline in students' academic self-rating is the largest change in student attitudes taking place between first and second year.

Figure 6.7: Changes in feelings of isolation

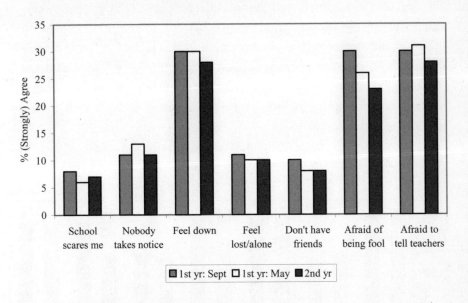

Table 6.2: Changes in student self-image over time

	First Year (Sept.)	First Year (May)	Second Year	Changes between First and Second Year
Academic self-rating	3.09	3.01	2.59	Decline (p<.001; -0.7 SD)
Good at sports	3.21	3.21	3.07	Decline (p<.001; -0.2 SD)
Body-image	3.10	2.99	2.94	No change
Popularity	3.25	3.20	3.12	Decline (p<.10; -0.1 SD)

Student perceptions of their own abilities become more negative over the course of first year with a further (and larger) decline during second year (see Table 6.2). Towards the end of second year, students are less likely to find their schoolwork easy, to feel they are working hard, to feel they are doing well and to be pleased with their schoolwork than they had been in first year (Figure 6.8). These patterns appear consistent with the view among many students that schoolwork is harder, and the workload more demanding, in second year than in first year (see Chapter Five). This decline in academic self-rating is evident across all groups of students with no significant variation by gender or ability group evident in the case-study schools. The one exception to this pattern is found among students who received learning support during first year. These students are less likely to have experienced a decline in their academic self-image, suggesting that learning support provision served to enhance their capacity to cope with schoolwork.

Figure 6.8: Changes in academic self-image

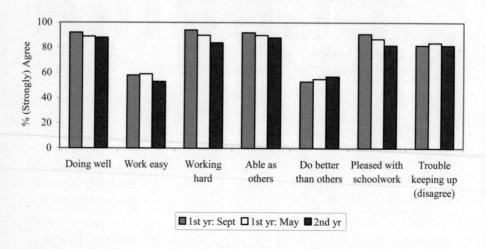

Figure 6.9 indicates trends in other aspects of student self-image. Students are less positive about their abilities in sports in second year than they were in first year (see also Table 6.2), a trend which is apparent across all groups of students. While there is some decline in student body-image over the course of first year, attitudes to their appearance appear to stabilise in second year. Students are somewhat less likely to report being liked by the rest of their class-mates in second year than in first year, though the difference is not marked.

Figure 6.9: Changes in self-image over time

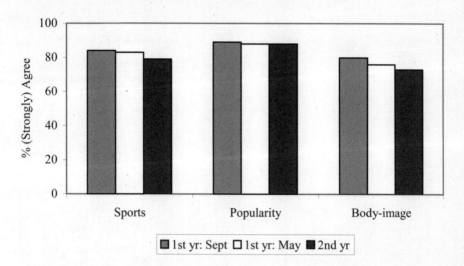

6.1.3 Changes in attitudes to school subjects and to learning

In addition to analysing changes in attitudes to school in general, it was possible to assess the extent to which trends emerged in student attitudes to specific school subjects, the pace of instruction within classes, student engagement in homework and access to learning support. In general, student attitudes to their school subjects are fairly stable over the course of first and second year (see Table 6.3); in other words, how students view subjects in first year is quite predictive of how they will assess these subjects in second year.

There is no evidence that some subjects are consistently seen as increasingly difficult as students move through the junior cycle. In the course of first year, students tend to see Science, French and Home Economics as becoming increasingly difficult. Four subjects, Maths, English, History and Business Studies, were seen as becoming more difficult in the course of second year.

The extent to which students find certain subjects interesting varies across subject areas (see Chapter Five) and these patterns do not alter substantially over time. Students become somewhat less interested in Science and Home Economics over the course of first year but slightly more interested in Maths. By the end of second year, students were somewhat less likely to find French, Materials Technology (Wood) and PE interesting than they had been in first year.

Table 6.3: Changes in attitudes to subject areas over time

	Changes over First Year	**Changes between First and Second Year**
Perceived difficulty		
Maths	No change	Increase (p<.001)
Science	Increase (p<.001)	No change
English	No change	Increase (p<.001)
History	No change	Increase (p<.001)
Geography	n.a.	No change
Home Economics	Increase (p<.01)	No change
Business Studies	n.a.	Increase (p<.10)
French	Increase (p<.01)	No change
Materials Technology	No change	No change
Art	n.a.	No change
Computers	No change	No change
Irish	No change	No change
PE	n.a.	No change
Perceived interest		
Maths	Increase (p<.05)	No change
Science	Decrease (p<.001)	No change
English	No change	No change
History	Increase (p<.10)	Decrease (p<.001)
Geography	n.a.	No change
Home Economics	Decrease (p<.01)	No change
Business Studies	n.a.	No change
French	No change	Decrease (p<.10)
Materials Technology	No change	Decrease (p<.10)
Art	n.a.	No change
Computers	No change	No change
Irish	No change	No change
PE	n.a.	Decrease (p<.01)

	Changes over First Year	**Changes between First and Second Year**
Perceived usefulness		
Maths	No change	No change
Science	Decrease (p<.01)	Decrease (p<.10)
English	No change	No change
History	Decrease (p<.01)	Decrease (p<.001)
Geography	n.a.	Decrease (p<.01)
Home Economics	No change	No change
Business Studies	n.a.	No change
French	No change	Decrease (p<.001)
Materials Technology	No change	No change
Art	n.a.	Decrease (p<.001)
Computers	No change	No change
Irish	No change	Decrease (p<.01)

Note: n.a. not applicable (data not collected at that time-point).

Again the extent to which students see their subjects as useful changes little over time. Over the course of first year, students were less likely to feel Science and History were useful, and between first and second year, students were less likely to find Geography, French, Art and Irish useful.

The study also allowed us to explore changes in student satisfaction with the overall pace of instruction and the pace in specific subjects between first and second year. There were no significant changes in students' overall perceptions of the pace of instruction between the end of first year and second year. At both waves of the survey, a fifth of students felt their teachers went too slowly while 31 per cent felt their teachers went too quickly. Similarly, there were no significant changes in student perceptions of the pace of instruction in English or Maths. In Irish and French, second year students were less likely to report that teachers went too quickly with their class than they had in first year while in Science students were more likely to report that teachers went too slowly with their class.

Figure 6.10: *Average amount of time spent on homework over time*

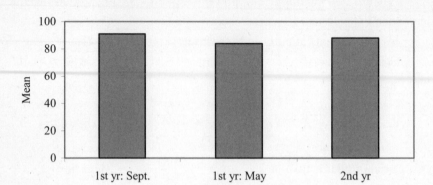

Chapter Five reported students' perceptions of the amount of homework received in second year compared with first year. The longitudinal nature of the study means that we can also assess the extent to which there are changes in the actual amount of time spent on homework and study among students in the case-study schools. Figure 6.10 indicates some decline in the amount of time spent on homework over the course of first year with average levels stabilising into second year.

Figure 6.11: *Proportion receiving learning support over time*

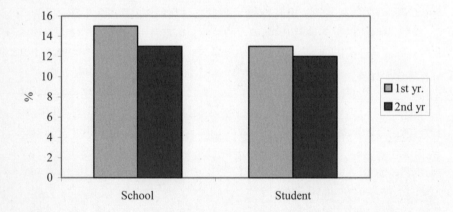

Figure 6.11 indicates trends in two measures of learning support for students: school reports of the numbers of students receiving formal learning

support[2] and student reports of the extent to which they had received extra help with their learning. There is a decline in the proportion of students receiving formal learning support indicating the targeting of provision towards students at entry to the school. However, there is no significant change in the proportion of students who report receiving extra help with their learning.

6.2 THE IMPACT OF FIRST YEAR EXPERIENCES ON ATTITUDES IN SECOND YEAR

This section looks at the extent to which student experiences in first year are predictive of how they get on in school in second year. The section focuses on the effect of three aspects of experience in first year: the transition into first year, the transition out of first year and attitudes to school in first year.

The ease of the transition to first year is found to have some longer term effects on students. Students who took longer to settle into first year are somewhat less positive about school in second year than those who settled in quickly, a pattern which holds for both male and female students. Similarly, those who settled in quickly (that is, within a week) are less likely to report feeling isolated in second year, a pattern which also holds for both boys and girls. However, student self-image in second year does not vary systematically according to the ease of transition to first year.

When schools with more and less strongly developed programmes to integrate students into first year are compared in relation to second year attitudes, very few differences are evident. Negative interaction with teachers is somewhat lower in 'high integration' schools while misbehaviour levels are higher in 'low integration' schools. Furthermore, students in high integration schools spend more time on homework in second year. As discussed in Chapter Two, schools with highly developed programmes for student integration in first year do not necessarily have strong support programmes for second year students; some schools may target provision to students making the transition to first year while for

---

[2] These data relate to nine of the case-study schools.

other schools support for first year students is located within a broader network of pastoral care for all students. There is no clear-cut relationship between having formalised support structures in second year and student attitudes to their teachers, with variation between schools also reflecting the social climate and the mixture of students within the school. However, levels of bullying are found to be generally lower in schools with more formalised support structure.

Chapter Four indicated that many students find schoolwork harder in second year than they had in first year. Difficulties in making the transition to second year are found to be associated with ease of transition into first year. Those who took longer to settle into post-primary education are more likely to find schoolwork in second year harder than that in first year; 57 per cent of students who took longer than a month to settle into post-primary education find it harder compared with 45 per cent of those who settled in more quickly. This pattern is more marked for male students than for female students. Similarly, the length of time taken to settle into first year is significantly related to whether respondents feel they spend more time on homework in second year than in first year (see Figure 6.12). This pattern is significant for male students but not for female students.

Figure 6.12: Amount of time spent on homework compared to first year by settling in period

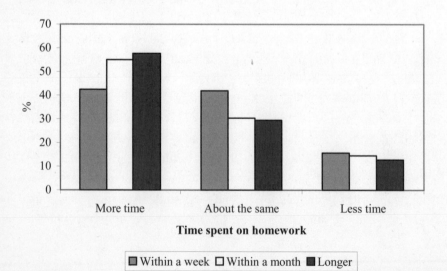

The relationship between ease of transition to second year and other attitudes to school was also explored. The most negative attitudes to school are found among those who find schoolwork easier in second year and spend less time on homework, indicating some disaffection and disengagement among this group. However, a decline in attitudes to school is evident among those who find schoolwork harder in second year. Similarly, the most negative attitudes to teachers are found among those who spend less time on homework in second year. These students also report less positive interaction with teachers and more negative interaction than other students. In contrast, feelings of isolation and anxiety are greater among those for whom second year represents an intensification of their school workload.

Tables 6.4a and 6.4b look at the effect of student attitudes in May of first year on outcomes in second year, controlling for gender, ability group and reading score in first year. It is clear that, across the measures (liking school, liking teachers, feeling isolated, academic self-image and body-image), attitudes at the end of first year are highly predictive of attitudes in second year; in other words, student attitudes in second year of the junior cycle are to a significant extent influenced by their experiences during the course of first year and the attitudes they form to school and to themselves at this stage.

Students who took longer to settle into post-primary education, that is, those who experienced transition difficulties on entry to first year, are more negative about school than students who settled in more quickly. Controlling for attitudes to school in first year, those in higher stream classes have more positive attitudes to school in second year; that is, their attitudes to school are more likely to have improved than those of other students. Furthermore, the quality of interaction between teachers and students impacts on student attitudes; students who have experienced praise and positive reinforcement from their teachers have more positive attitudes to school while those who have been given out to frequently by teachers have more negative attitudes to school.

Table 6.4a: Influence of first year experiences on second year attitudes

	Liking school			Liking teachers			Feelings of isolation		
	(1)	(2)	(3)	(1)	(2)	(3)	(1)	(2)	(3)
Constant	2.449	1.100	1.137	2.799	1.024	0.971	1.508	0.571	0.517
Female	0.077	-0.025	-0.026	0.168*	0.080	0.083	0.088	0.113*	0.115*
Higher stream class	0.009	0.124◆	0.121◆	-0.109	0.114	0.118	0.033	0.027	0.033
Middle stream class	0.039	0.071	0.063	-0.052	-0.033	-0.034	-0.031	0.017	0.035
Lower stream class	-0.106	-0.032	-0.049	0.109	0.166	0.179	0.031	0.152	0.187◆
(Base: Mixed ability)									
Reading score (1st year)	0.002	-0.001	0.001	-0.001	-0.002	-0.002	0.003◆	0.004**	0.004*
Transition difficulties (1st year)	-0.147◆	0.019	0.023	0.001	0.095	0.096	0.160*	-0.108◆	-0.113◆
First year attitudes:									
Liking school		0.518***	0.518***		-	-		-	
Liking teachers		-			0.482***	0.487***		-	-
Isolation		-	-		-	-		0.528***	0.515***
Positive teacher interaction		0.073◆	0.068◆		0.090*	0.095*		-0.073*	-0.065◆
Negative teacher interaction		-0.078**	-0.079**		-0.014	-0.017		-0.023	-0.021
Being bullied		0.005	0.004		-0.074	-0.075		0.135*	0.147*
Academic self-rating		-0.012	-0.012		0.089	0.091◆		0.029	0.027
Transition to 2nd year:									
Work easier			-0.018			0.155			-0.016
Work harder			-0.051			0.053			0.100*
(Base: About the same)									
Adjusted R²	0.004	0.341	0.340	0.015	0.339	0.340	0.019	0.340	0.345

Note: *** p<.001, ** p<.01, * p<.05, ◆ p<.10.

Table 6.4b: Influence of first year experiences on second year attitudes (continued)

	Academic self-image			Body-image			Third-level aspirations (logistic regression)		
	(1)	(2)	(3)	(1)	(2)	(3)	(1)	(2)	(3)
Constant	2.598	1.186	1.270	3.124	1.749	1.730	-1.839***	-4.095***	-4.256***
Female	-0.033	-0.055	-0.055	-0.425***	-0.207*	-0.205*	0.266	0.202	0.196
Higher stream class	0.012	0.050	0.043	0.083	0.175◆	0.177◆	0.551	0.662◆	0.677◆
Middle stream class	0.081	0.021	-0.008	0.282*	0.286**	0.286**	0.218	0.134	0.194
Lower stream class	0.212◆	0.172◆	0.125	0.163	0.317◆	0.322◆	-0.326	-0.260	-0.174
(Base: Mixed ability)									
Reading score (1st yr)	0.003***	0.002◆	0.002◆	-0.003	-0.001	-0.001	0.070***	0.065***	0.064***
Transition difficulties (1st yr)	-0.087	0.017	0.033	0.014	0.140	0.140	0.198	0.318	0.278
First year attitudes:									
Academic self-image		0.461***	0.465***		-0.007	-0.005		0.595***	0.596*
Body image		-	-		0.453***	0.454***		-	-
Positive teacher interaction		0.137***	0.126***		-0.001	0.001		0.341◆	0.352◆
Negative teacher interaction		-0.071**	-0.077***		0.053	0.052		-0.211	-0.201
Being bullied		0.006	0.003		-0.198**	-0.198*		0.185	0.210
Transition to 2nd year:									
Work easier			0.122◆			0.052			-0.369
Work harder			-0.124***			0.021			0.253
(Base: About the same)									
Adjusted R²	0.033	0.408	0.425	0.090	0.330	0.328	0.176	0.210	0.214

Note: *** p<.001, ** p<.01, * p<.05, ◆ p<.10.

In relation to attitudes to teachers, female students are more likely to like their teachers than their male counterparts, all else being equal. As with attitudes to school, students who have experienced positive interaction with their teachers in first year are more likely to have more positive attitudes to their teachers in second year. Furthermore, students who had more positive views of their own academic abilities in first year are more likely to have positive attitudes to their teachers.

Students who experienced transition difficulties in first year are more likely to report feelings of isolation and anxiety in second year. Perhaps surprisingly, such feelings are more commonly reported among students with higher reading scores; this may reflect more study-related pressure and anxiety among this group (see Hannan et al., 1996, on stress levels among students). Female students are more likely to report feeling isolated or anxious than their male counterparts, controlling for their attitudes to school in first year. Again the social climate of the school and class plays a role in this respect; positive interaction with teachers is found to reduce student isolation while having experienced bullying in first year is associated with an increased prevalence of such feelings. Over and above the effect of transition difficulties in first year, students who experience difficulties in making the transition to second year, that is, those who find schoolwork harder in second year than in first year, are more likely to report feelings of isolation and anxiety.

As might be expected, students with higher reading scores have a more positive view of their academic abilities and their capacity to cope with schoolwork. Perhaps surprisingly, students in lower stream classes have more positive academic self-images than those in other class types; this may be related to the reference group they use, that is, they are comparing themselves with other students in a lower stream class and to the slower pace of instruction reported by some students in these classes (see Chapter Five). Students who have received praise or positive reinforcement from teachers have a more positive view of their own abilities while those who have been given out to or criticised by teachers have a more negative self-image. The nature of the transition to second year is predictive of student academic self-image with more positive views among those who find schoolwork easier and more negative views among those who find schoolwork in second year more difficult.

Female students are found to have a more negative view of their own appearance than male counterparts, even controlling for body-image in first year, indicating a widening gender gap in self-image. Students in streamed schools appear to have more positive body-images than those in other schools, a pattern which is most likely related to the social composition of the schools rather than to streaming per se. Those who experienced bullying in first year have a more negative view of their appearance in second year; this is likely to reflect the targeting of aspects of a student's appearance in other students jeering or mocking them, a pattern which is consistent with previous research (see Hannan et al., 1996).

The final model in Table 6.4b looks at the factors predicting educational aspirations in second year. Students in higher stream classes are more likely than those in other class groups to aspire to third-level education, all else being equal. As might be expected, students with higher reading scores are also more likely to say they plan to go on to college as are students with a more positive view of their own abilities. Those who have received praise or positive reinforcement from their teachers are significantly more likely than other students to aspire to third-level education.

In sum, student experiences in second year are strongly influenced by the attitudes formed in their first year of post-primary education. In addition, the nature of the transition into first year and from first year into second year has a formative influence on student attitudes. Aspects of school and classroom climate, particularly the extent of positive interaction with teachers, are associated with more positive attitudes to school and to themselves among second year students.

6.3 CONCLUSIONS

This chapter has looked at changes in student attitudes in the case-study schools over the course of first and second year in the junior cycle. In keeping with international research (Doddington et al., 1999; Macbeath and Mortimore, 2001), attitudes to school become more negative over time with less positive attitudes evident among students in second year than among the same students in first year. Furthermore, the interaction between teachers and students appears to become more negative while student misbehaviour tends to increase, in keeping with the views expressed by key personnel in Chapter Two. There is evidence of a gender gap emerging with male students becoming more negative than their female counterparts in their view of school. There is a certain stability in student attitudes to school subjects, indicating that students' initial experiences of a subject may have longer term effects. However, certain subjects are seen as becoming more difficult and less interesting over time.

Student experiences in first year and the attitudes that are formed as a result of these experiences are found to be highly predictive of how they fare in second year. In particular, the social climate of the school shapes student attitudes with positive teacher-student interaction associated with more positive views of school and teachers, more positive academic self-image, reduced feelings of isolation and anxiety, and higher educational aspirations. The nature of the transition between school years also has an effect; students who had difficulties settling into first year are less likely to like school and more likely to feel isolated in second year. In addition, those who find schoolwork harder in second year than in first year are more likely to feel isolated and have more negative views of their own abilities than other students.

Chapter Seven

CONCLUSIONS

This study set out to capture how students experience their second year in the junior cycle. In so doing, it builds upon research on the experiences of students making the transition from primary to post-primary education (Smyth et al., 2004). International research has highlighted the importance of taking account of the 'student voice' and the potential contribution of the student perspective to school improvement and policy development more generally (Macbeath et al., 2001; Rudduck and Flutter, 2004a). Listening to the student voice as part of this study allows us to gain a unique insight into the issues which are important to students themselves as a basis for policy development. Consulting students may be especially beneficial in the middle years when, as international research suggests, students' motivation and engagement in school life may 'dip' (Rudduck and Flutter, 2004a). The study draws on rich information, both quantitative and qualitative, to explore young people's experience of the 'middle year' in the junior cycle. In order to provide a holistic view of the junior cycle within schools, student accounts are placed in the context of the perspectives of the key personnel working with second year students. This chapter presents the main findings of the study and highlights issues for future policy development.

7.1 SCHOOL AND CLASSROOM CLIMATE AND SUPPORT STRUCTURES FOR SECOND YEAR STUDENTS

The twelve case-study schools vary markedly in their support structures for second year students. However, the Class Tutor and/or Year Head system represents the cornerstone of provision across all of the schools.

The most marked variation between schools occurs in relation to the involvement of Guidance Counsellors and other pastoral care staff and in the extent to which support structures are integrated to bring about a whole-school approach. Many of the key personnel are generally satisfied with the supports they can offer their second year students. Nevertheless, key personnel in all schools feel that there are ways in which supports for students in the school could be improved. The main suggestions for change include the provision of external psychological support services, improved guidance provision for students within the school and having greater resources available for home-school liaison.

The presence of formal support structures cannot in itself explain the extent to which students avail of such supports within the school, however. For example, the willingness of second year students to approach their teachers with a problem or to talk to a teacher about bullying is not clearly related to the prevalence of support structures for second year students within the school. Neither are strongly developed supports sufficient to ensure more positive interactions and fewer negative interactions between teachers and students within the school. It is therefore important to consider the effect of the informal climate within the school on student experiences.

The findings of the study indicate that the informal atmosphere of the school has a significant influence on how students fare in second year. Students are more likely to approach a teacher with an academic problem if they have previously had positive interaction with them. They are also more likely to like school and teachers if they have had positive interaction with their teachers. The reverse situation is also true in that students who feel they have been constantly 'given out to' or treated unfairly by their teachers are more disengaged from school life and less likely to approach school personnel when they have difficulties. Therefore, the types of interactions students have with their teachers may have as much, if not more, influence than the formal support structures that schools put in place for their students. Fostering good relations within the school environment is thus as important as putting formal structures in place for students.

The nature of the school climate is also relevant in terms of school discipline. Being frequently given out to by teachers is associated with more negative attitudes to school and many sanctions, even more serious interventions such as suspension from school, are seen as ineffective by many students in the case-study schools. Promoting positive reinforcement and rewarding positive behaviour on the part of students may therefore be a more useful tool in dealing with discipline issues and in fostering a positive school climate.

The nature of relations among students in the school also has important consequences for how students fare in second year. Students who have experienced bullying at school are more likely to feel isolated or anxious and have more negative perceptions of themselves than other students. Typically bullying tends to be dealt with as a discipline problem in the case-study schools, the exception being in Belmore Street where a more pastoral approach to the issue is taken. Treating bullying as a purely disciplinary issue does not appear to be effective, however, for two reasons. Firstly, only a very small minority of students who have been bullied talk to any of the school personnel about it and students are much more reliant on friends and family in such circumstances. Secondly, some staff are themselves ambiguous about what constitutes bullying, emphasising more visible forms such as physical bullying and downplaying less visible forms, such as students being excluded, forms which students themselves may find more upsetting. It is important, therefore, that anti-bullying policies are located within a broader climate designed to foster positive relations within the school.

The importance of formal support structures being underpinned by a positive school climate is perhaps best illustrated by looking at two contrasting schools. Dixon Street School, a coeducational school with designated disadvantaged status, has a strong emphasis on student integration measures in first year and maintains fairly extensive supports for second year students. However, students report high levels of negative interaction with teachers, many feel that teachers treat different groups of students unequally and many students, especially in the lower streams, are disaffected with school and consequently have high levels of misbehaviour. In contrast, the informal environment in Belmore Street school, a girls' school which was mixed in intake, is one of the most positive in the study. Students in this school have the lowest level of negative interactions with their teachers, are much less likely to report that students are treated unequally, have the lowest rate of bullying and misbehaviour and the best inter-student relations of all of the case-study schools.

In policy terms, it is important that schools should be encouraged to put in place developed and integrated support structures for all junior cycle students. However, these structures are unlikely to be effective in promoting personal and social development among students unless they are underpinned by a positive school and classroom climate. It is important that school development planning takes account not only of the improvement of formal policies but also includes measures to promote student involvement and engagement. Schools should be encouraged to promote student involvement in the school at an informal level, through sports and other extracurricular activities, and at a formal level through student councils or other consultative structures. It is important too that any measures designed to listen to the 'student voice' should incorporate junior cycle as well as senior cycle students and should endeavour to involve a broad array of students, not just those who are already more engaged in school life.

In developing support structures for students, it is important to recognise that choices made on the part of students and their parents mean that Irish post-primary schools differ markedly in the socio-economic and ability profile of their student intake (Smyth, 1999; Smyth et al., 2004). Previous research has indicated that students attending schools serving predominantly working-class populations tend to achieve lower academic grades and are more likely to leave school early, all else being equal (Smyth, 1999). This study provides some further insight into the processes shaping these outcomes. Among the case-study schools, students in predominantly working-class schools tend to have more negative attitudes to school and their teachers and are less likely to see their schoolwork as becoming increasingly challenging as they move through junior cycle. The effect of a concentration of students with more negative attitudes to school in a particular context may be compounded to some extent by the greater prevalence of streaming in designated disadvantaged schools (see below). It is vital in policy terms that these schools are provided with the support to develop measures to increase student engagement and they are helped to build on the already high levels of positive interaction between teachers and students to promote positive behaviour and reduce negative interaction.

7.2 TEACHING AND LEARNING IN SECOND YEAR

7.2.1 Subject choice and attitudes to subjects in second year

The case-study schools varied markedly in their approach to subject choice with the result that students differed a good deal in the number of subjects they were exposed to in first year according to the school they attended. By second year, students had chosen their subject and so there was much less variation in the number of subjects taken, though some differences between schools remained. In general, students with learning difficulties and those from minority groups tended to take fewer subjects, reflecting an exemption from studying Irish for some students and the withdrawal of students from certain subjects for additional learning support. Contrary to recent discussions of 'curriculum overload', there was no evidence that taking more subjects was associated with more academic difficulties or more negative attitudes to school.

In keeping with their preferences in first year, second year students tend to favour subjects with a more practical orientation to more traditional 'academic' subjects and are more likely to find these subjects interesting. In general, second year students tend to see the subjects they take as useful, with the exception of Irish and History. However, many students find the more academic subjects, particularly the languages, Maths and Science, difficult. Furthermore, students feel that too little time is devoted to Physical Education and Computer Studies in second year.

A more general issue emerged in terms of restrictions on subject choice for second years with over half of the students reporting that there are subjects they would have liked to be taking but aren't currently taking. Generally, the subjects they wanted to take were the more practically oriented ones and they could not do so because the subject was not provided in the school as a whole or was not made available to their class group (typically the middle or lower streams). Unsurprisingly, students who report restricted subject choice or who regret taking certain subjects have significantly more negative attitudes to school and to their teachers than other groups of students. In terms of subject choice, therefore, it is important that student access to the more practically oriented subjects be facilitated at the school and class level. The provision of a greater practical orientation within the more 'academic' subjects may also provide a basis for engaging students in school life.

As well as differentiating between the different subject options, by second year even mixed ability schools had grouped students into different ability classes for some subjects, usually Maths, Irish and English. The case-study schools varied in the amount of flexibility offered to students in selecting their subject levels. As a result, considerable variation is apparent between schools in the proportion taking higher or foundation level, controlling for prior ability among students. It is important that schools should endeavour to facilitate as many students as feasible in taking subjects at as high a level as possible. Given the strong relationship between subject levels at junior cycle and those at Leaving Certificate level, overly restrictive access to higher level subjects is likely to contribute to underperformance among students and may affect their longer term educational and career options.

7.2.2 What helps students to learn

When second year students are asked about the kind of teaching and lessons which help them to learn, the single most frequently mentioned characteristic is that the teacher explains things clearly. The importance of the informal climate in the school and particularly the relationship between teachers and students within the classroom environment is also crucial in enhancing student learning. Having a helpful or friendly teacher, and being able to talk to or have fun with the teacher are seen as strongly positive influences on student learning. Another important factor is intrinsic interest in the subject on the part of both students and teachers; students tend to report that they find it easier to learn in classes where they themselves like the subject and/or are good at the subject but they also find it easier to learn where the teacher obviously enjoys teaching the subject. Only a minority of students describe more traditional 'chalk and talk' methods as helping them to learn. Interestingly, it is students in the lower streams and those from working class backgrounds that tend to prefer teacher-led lessons.

A considerable proportion of second year students express dissatisfaction with the pace of instruction in their classes; over a quarter of second year students in the case-study schools feel that their teachers go too slowly with their class while almost a third feel that teachers go too quickly. It is clear that differentiation in the work assigned and methods used in response to differing student needs and abilities is not occurring in many classrooms. It is important that teachers are given appropriate support and training in working with mixed ability classes in such a way that maximises the learning of all students. Difficulties with pace of instruction are not only evident in mixed ability schools, however. Students in lower stream classes are not being adequately challenged in terms of schoolwork and are most likely to feel that teachers go too slowly in their lessons, a pattern which may contribute to lack of engagement in class and hence misbehaviour.

The majority of second year students feel that homework and tests help them to learn. However, there is a certain degree of anxiety around tests evident on the part of students. Students who rate themselves as academically 'above average' are more likely to find that homework and tests help them to learn than students who rate themselves as 'below average'. Students who agree that homework helps them to learn actually do spend more time on their homework indicating that they feel this is a productive way of learning. Those who are spending the most amount of time doing homework in second year are female students, those who rate themselves as 'above average' and those in mixed ability classes.

In sum, from the student perspective, effective teaching requires clarity of explanation, teacher approachability and an appropriate pace of instruction. Taking subjects which the student enjoys is also seen as the key to effective learning. Traditional 'chalk and talk' approaches are generally less popular with students, indicating the need to adopt a greater variety of teaching methods in junior cycle classrooms. However, it should be recognised that not all students (particularly those in lower streams and those who rate themselves as below average academically) may feel comfortable in moving away from a teacher-led format and that the teaching methods adopted should take account of students' interests and abilities. Relations between teachers and students emerge as key in student learning. Building up good relations between teachers and students in the classroom context is also likely to prove the foundation for a positive climate across the school as a whole.

7.2.3 Student engagement in schoolwork

In looking at student engagement in schoolwork in second year, it is clear that two distinct groups of students have emerged: those who experience second year as an intensification of their academic involvement and those who are drifting or even actively disengaging from schoolwork. The first group tends to find schoolwork harder in second year than in first year and is spending more time on homework than previously. This group is disproportionately made up of female students, those from professional, other non-manual and farming backgrounds, those with higher academic ability levels and those in mixed ability or higher stream classes.

In contrast, the students who are disengaging from schoolwork are disproportionately from the lower stream classes, those with lower ability levels, those who rate their academic ability as 'below average' and those from working class backgrounds. It would appear that students in the lower streams may not be adequately challenged in their classes. Many find that the pace of instruction is too slow and they are more likely than other groups to find schoolwork actually getting easier in second year. They are also more likely to say they are doing less homework than they did in first year and are spending less time on their homework than students in the higher stream classes.

International research had indicated a general disengagement in schoolwork in the 'middle years' (see Doddington et al., 1999; Rudduck and Flutter, 2004a). However, it is clear from this study that important divergences take place in the learning trajectories of students in second year, with some students intensifying their academic engagement while others drift or actively disengage from school life. Of particular concern in policy terms is that this process is allied to increasing social differentiation with a widening gap in student experiences on the basis of gender, ability, social class background and ability group. If such differences continue into the third year of the junior cycle, they are likely to have important consequences for educational participation and performance among students.

7.2.4 Peer influences on learning

The perceived influence of peers on students' engagement in schoolwork appears somewhat contradictory, with students trying to balance on the fine line between wanting to appear clever and not wanting to be seen as a 'show-off'. Half of the students in the case-study schools state that it is important for them to be seen as clever in their class but over half report that they don't like people who want to show they're clever in class. Being studious is seen as acceptable as long as it is not seen as 'showing off'. Students sometimes lie about how hard they are studying not only in case they do badly in tests or exams but also so that other students will not tease them about being 'swots'. It may be that students want to be seen as 'naturally' clever by their peer group rather than as having worked to achieve.

Students who rate themselves as 'below average' academically appear to be the most strongly influenced by their peer group. These students are more reliant on their peer group for their identity rather than academic achievement. They are more likely than other students to say that being part of a group is more important to them than doing well, that they don't like people who show they're clever in class and are more likely to pretend they haven't studied for an exam so they won't look stupid if they do badly. It is hard to disentangle the causal relationship at play here; students may seek refuge in a group identity as a compensation for school failure or alternatively academic underperformance may be the result of students being more involved in social than academic activities.

International research highlights that students' involvement with their peer group as opposed to schoolwork increases during the middle years with negative implications for their academic engagement and performance (Hargreaves, 1996; Erikson, 1968, Anderman and Maehr, 1994; Wenz-Gross and Siperstein, 1998; Cotterell, 1996; Goodenow, 1993). However, findings from this study indicate a more contradictory role for the peer group with students trying to balance doing well at schoolwork with not being a 'show-off'. In keeping with previous studies (see, for example, Willis, 1977), the peer effect is found to be strongest among students who rate themselves as below average academically. However, it is worth noting that students across the board, even those who are disaffected with school life, seem to consider the attainment of qualifications as important.

7.3 THE IDENTITY OF SECOND YEAR STUDENTS

International research suggests that student engagement with school and levels of motivation dip during the 'middle years' (Doddington et al., 1999; Harris and Rudduck, 1993). The findings of this study indicate that student attitudes to school life do, in fact, decline in second year compared with first year; second year students are less positive about school, less positive about their teachers, are less likely to receive praise from their teachers and are more likely to be given out to by teachers. Furthermore, some aspects of student self-image decline over time; in particular, students feel less confident in their ability to handle their schoolwork in second year than they had in first year.

From the staff perspective, second year is seen as generally the most difficult year in the junior cycle. Key personnel in the case-study schools feel that second year students are more disruptive than other year groups and often try to 'test' the school system. Bullying is seen as potentially more likely to occur in second year than among other year groups. Staff attribute these changes in student behaviour, on the one hand, to developmental changes happening during adolescence and, on the other hand, to the lack of a structured exam focus in second year. On the basis of student responses, it is clear that (with the exception of school absenteeism) all forms of misbehaviour and related punishment increase between first and second year. In particular, messing in class becomes quite a frequent activity and the incidence of skipping classes, or 'mitching', also increases. However, in contrast to the views of staff, no significant change occurs in the prevalence of bullying.

This study is in line with previous research indicating a disimprovement in student attitudes as they move through the school system, a pattern which applies across all levels of ability. However, it is important to note that, while such a trend is evident on average, important differences are evident between different groups of students. Within coeducational schools, male students report a greater incidence of misbehaviour, more negative interaction with teachers and are less likely to like school in second year than their female counterparts. The informal climate of the school emerges as a key factor in maintaining positive attitudes to school. Students who have experienced praise or positive feedback from their teachers improve their perceptions of school life, of teachers and their own capacity as learners, and are less likely to feel isolated or anxious in the school context. Awareness of the potential 'dips' in student motivation as they move through the school system and of the importance of classroom climate in facilitating student engagement should therefore be incorporated into initial and on-going teacher education programmes.

Second year students must be seen not only in terms of where they have come from (their experiences of first year) but also in terms of where they are going – their orientation to the Junior Certificate along with longer-term educational and career aspirations. By March of second year, teachers within the case-study schools have started to talk about the Junior Certificate exam. However, students themselves are divided between feeling it is too early to think about the Junior Certificate and those who consider they should be thinking about it (even though they may not be actively studying at this stage). The majority of second year classes in the case-study schools view the Junior Certificate exam as important.

The majority of students in the case-study schools expect to go on to third-level education with higher aspirations evident among certain groups of students. Female students and those from higher professional backgrounds have the highest aspirations with the lowest aspirations found among students with lower reading and maths scores, those who rate themselves as 'below average' academically as well as among the lower stream classes. Students in the case-study schools also have relatively high occupational aspirations with most aspiring towards professional occupations. Occupational aspirations are closely tied to the social background of the students and to their academic self-image, with the highest aspirations among those from professional backgrounds, those with higher ability levels and those who view themselves as academically above average.

7.4 VARIATION IN SCHOOL EXPERIENCES ACROSS GROUPS OF STUDENTS

7.4.1 Ability grouping

The *Moving Up* study indicated significant effects of streaming on the ease of transition into post-primary education as well as on student attitudes to school and academic progress during first year (Smyth et al., 2004). Ability grouping continues to have an effect on the experiences of students in second year, particularly on students' academic experiences. Students in the lower streams appear to be less challenged academically than their counterparts in other types of class groups. They find the pace of instruction too slow in their classes and generally find schoolwork easier in second year than they did in first year. They say they are doing less homework; in some cases when they are interviewed, they report doing no homework. Students in the lower streams also feel more restricted in terms of subject choice. Students in lower stream classes have more negative attitudes towards school and have the lowest educational aspirations, with a significant proportion expecting to finish school before the Leaving Certificate. It is not surprising, therefore, that students in lower streams are disproportionately found in the group of students that appear to be disengaging from school life. Streaming may also serve to increase social inequality in terms of academic engagement and performance because it is used disproportionately in designated disadvantaged schools (see Smyth et al., 2004). Given the effects of streaming on student disengagement, it is important that schools should be encouraged to develop more flexible forms of ability grouping and be supported in so doing by the provision of professional development in relation to mixed ability teaching methods. Within initial teacher education, students should also be made aware of the potential impact of streaming and supported in utilising mixed ability teaching methods.

7.4.2 Gender

Clear gender differences are emerging among students in second year. Male students tend to have more negative interaction with their teachers and misbehaviour is more common among male students. Female students are generally more positive in their attitudes to school and their teachers than their male counterparts in the same school context; this gender gap in attitudes to school widens between first and second year. Male students are more likely to think that it is important for them to be seen as clever by their classmates but, on the other hand, they are also more likely to think that being part of the group is more important than doing well at school. In overall terms, male students are less likely than their female counterparts to be intensifying their academic engagement in schoolwork and are more likely to be 'drifting' or even actively disengaging.

Clear gender differences are also evident in terms of aspirations for the future. Female students have higher academic goals than their male counterparts in general. Nevertheless, female students generally have more gendered notions of the household division of labour with female students saying they would be most likely to work part-time while their partner worked full-time. Similarly, female students are less likely than their male counterparts to aspire to higher professional occupations and more likely to aspire to lower professional jobs, mainly in traditionally female occupational niches.

A good deal of debate has taken place internationally about the factors influencing male underperformance in post-primary education (see, for example, Arnot, 2002; Epstein et al., 1998; Ellwood, 2002). This study indicates a widening gender gap in second year in terms of engagement in school life and schoolwork with greater disaffection evident among male students. This gap is likely to contribute to male underperformance and early school leaving in the future. It could be argued that general policy measures to enhance student engagement, for example, through promoting a positive school climate, rewarding positive behaviour rather than utilising negative sanctions and providing students with access to subjects with a more practical orientation, would have positive benefits for (groups of) male students. Given the profile of schools that stream students on the basis of ability, a move towards mixed ability base classes is likely to benefit all students but particularly male students.

In conclusion, the second year of the junior cycle has often been characterised as one in which students 'drift'. However, the findings of this study indicate that second year may be a crucial year in terms of student engagement. An important distinction is evident between students for whom second year represents an intensification of their academic effort and those who are drifting or even actively disengaging from schoolwork. This distinction reflects and reinforces differentiation in terms of gender, social class, prior ability level and ability group, with female students, those from middle-class backgrounds, those with higher ability levels and those in mixed ability or higher stream classes more likely to become increasingly engaged academically. The informal climate of the school and classroom, that is, the quality of relations between teachers and students and among students themselves, is found to play a key role in enhancing student engagement in school life at this stage in the junior cycle. The extent to which students' experiences in second year influence how they fare subsequently is the subject of ongoing research.

REFERENCES

Anderman, E. M. and Maehr, M. L. 1994, "Motivation and schooling in the middle grades", *Review of Educational Research*, vol. 64, no. 2, pp. 287-309.

Andersson, B. E. 1996, "Why am I in school? A study of Swedish adolescents' perceptions of their school situation", *EERA Bulletin*, July, p. 17-23.

Brookover, W., Beady, C., Flood, P., Schweitzer, J., Wisenbaker, J. 1979, *School Social Systems and Student Achievement: Schools Can Make a Difference*, New York: Praeger.

Conway, P. 2002, "Learning in communities of practice: rethinking teaching and learning in disadvantaged contexts", *Irish Educational Studies*, vol. 21, no. 3, pp. 61-91.

Cotterell, J. 1996, *Social Networks and Social Influences in Adolescence,* London: Routledge.

Devine, D. 2004, "School matters - listening to what children have to say," in *Primary voices: Equality, Diversity and Childhood in Irish Primary Schools*, J. Deegan, D. Devine, and A. Lodge, eds., Dublin: Institute of Public Administration, pp. 109-127.

Doddington, C., Flutter, J., and Rudduck, J. 1999, "Exploring and Explaining 'Dips' in Motivation and Performance in Primary and Secondary Schooling", *Research in Education*, vol. 61, pp. 29-38.

Duffield, J., Allan, J., Turner, E., and Morris, B. 2000, "Pupils' Voices on Achievement: An alternative to the standards agenda", *Cambridge Journal of Education*, vol. 30, no. 2, pp. 263-274.

Eccles, J. S., Midgley, C., Wigfield, A., Buchanan, C. M., Reuman, D. A., Flanagan, C., and MacIver, D. 1993, "Development during Adolescence. The Impact of Stage-Environment Fit on Young Adolescents' Experiences in Schools and in Families", *American Psychologist*, vol. 48, no. 2, pp. 90-101.

Erikson, E. 1968, *Identity, Youth and Crisis,* New York: Norton.

Fielding, M. 2004, "Transformative approaches to student voice: theoretical underpinnings, recalcitrant realities", *British Educational Research Journal*, vol. 30, no. 2, pp. 295-311.

Fletcher A. 2003, *Unleashing student voice: Research supporting meaningful student involvement*, Olympia, WA: The Feechild Project. (www.educationaalliance.org)

Flutter, J. and Rudduck, J. 2004, *Consulting Pupils: What's in it for schools?*, London: Routledge.

Galton, M., Gray, J., and Rudduck, J. 2003, *Transfer and Transitions in the Middle Years of Schooling (7-14): Continuities and Discontinuities in Learning*, Queen's Printer, University of Cambridge, Research Report no. 443.

Goodenow, C. 1993, "Classroom Belonging Among Early Adolescent Students: Relationships to Motivation and Achievement", *Journal of Early Adolescence*, vol. 13, pp. 21-24.

Gorard, S. with Taylor, C. 2004, *Combining Methods in Educational and Social Research*, Buckingham: Open University Press.

Gray, J., Hopkins, D., Reynolds, D., Farrell, S., and Jesson, D. 1999, *Improving Schools: Performance and Potential*, Buckingham: Open University Press.

Hallam, S. and Ireson, J. 2005, "Secondary school teachers' pedagogic practices when teaching mixed and structured ability classes", *Research Papers in Education*, vol. 20, no. 1, pp. 3-24.

Hannan, D. F., Smyth, E., McCullagh, J., O'Leary, R., McMahon, D. 1996, *Co-education and Gender Equality: Exam Performance, Stress and Personal Development*, Dublin: Oak Tree Press/ESRI.

Hargreaves, A. 1996, "Revisiting voice", *Researcher*, vol. 25, no. 1, pp. 12-19.

Harris, S. and Rudduck, J. 1993, "Establishing the seriousness of learning in the early years of secondary schooling", *British Journal of Educational Psychology*, vol. 63, no. 2, pp. 322-336.

Holdsworth, R. and Thomson, P. 2001, "Options within the regulation and containment of 'student voice' and/or Students researching and acting for change: Australian Experiences", Student Voice Symposium, American Educational Research Association, New Orleans.

Jackson, D., Raymond, L., Weatherill, L. and Fielding, M. 1998, *Students as Researchers*. Paper presented at ICSEI, Manchester. (http://www.leadership. fau.edu/ICSEI/htm Downloaded 9 March 2005)

Johnson, B. and Turner, L.A. 2003, "Data collection strategies in mixed methods research", in Tashakorri, A. and Teddlie, C. (eds.) *Handbook of Mixed Methods in Social and Behavioral Research*, California: Sage, pp. 297-319.

Kordalewski, J. 1999, *Incorporating Student Voice into Teaching Practice*, ERIC Digest.

Kroeger, S., Burton, C., Comarata, A., Combs, C., Hamm, J.C., Hopkins, R. and Kouche, B. 2004, "Student voice and critical reflection", *Helping Students at Risk, Teaching Exceptional Children*, vol. 36, no. 3, pp 50-57.

Lee, P. Statuto, C., and Kedar-Voivodas, G. 1983, "Elementary school children's perceptions of their actual and ideal school experience", *Journal of Education and Psychology*, vol. 75, no. 6, pp. 838-47.

Lynch, K. 1999, *Equality in Education*, Dublin: Gill and Macmillan

Lynch, K. and Lodge, A. 2002, *Equality and Power in Schools. Redistribution, Recognition and Representation*, London: Routledge Falmer.

Lyons, M., Lynch, K., Sheerin, E., Close, S. and Boland, P. 2003, *Inside Classrooms: The Teaching and Learning of Mathematics in Social Context*, Dublin: IPA.

Macbeath, J., Myers, K., and Demetriou, H. 2001, "Supporting Teachers in Consulting Pupils about Aspects of Teaching and Learning, and Evaluating Impact", *Forum*, vol. 43, no. 2, pp. 78-82.

Macbeath, J. and Mortimore, J. 2001, *Improving School Effectiveness*, Buckingham: Open University Press.

Maden, M. and Rudduck, J. 1997, "Listen to the learners", *Times Educational Supplement*, 4 July.

Millar, D. and Kelly, D. 1999, *From Junior to Leaving Certificate: A Longitudinal Study of 1994 Junior Certificate Candidates who took the Leaving Certificate Examination in 1997*, Dublin, NCCA/ERC.

Morgan, D.L. 1996, "Focus groups", *Annual Review of Sociology*, vol. 22, pp. 129-152.

National Children's Office 2002, *The National Children's Strategy*, Dublin, National Children's Office. (http://www.nco.ie/national_childrens_strategy/)

O'Brien, M. 2004, *Making the Move. Students', Teachers' and Parents' Perspectives of Transfer from First to Second-level Schooling*, Dublin: Marino Institute of Education.

Osborn, M. 2001, "Constants and Contexts in Pupil Experience of Learning and Schooling: Comparing Learners in England, France and Denmark", *Comparative Education*, vol. 37, no. 3, pp. 267-278.

Rudduck, J. 2002, "The SERA Lecture 2002: The Transformative Potential of Consulting Young People about Teaching, Learning and Schooling", *Scottish Educational Review*, vol. 34, no. 2, pp. 123-137.

Rudduck, J. and Flutter, J. 2004, *How to Improve Your School. Giving Pupils a Voice*, London, New York: Continuum.

Rudduck, J. and Flutter, J. 2004, *Challenge of year 8: Sustaining Pupils' Engagement with Learning*, Cambridge: Pearson Publishing.

Rudduck, J., Chaplain, R., and Wallace, G. 1996, *School Improvement: What Can Pupils Tell Us?*, London: David Fulton.

Rutter, M., Maughan, B., Mortimore, P. and Ouston, J. 1979, *Fifteen Thousand Hours: Secondary Schools and their Effects on Children*, London: Open Books.

Sammons, P., Hillman, J., and Mortimore, P. 2004, *Key Characteristics of Effective School*, London: David Fulton.

Smith, D.J. and Tomlinson, S. 1989, *The School Effect: A Study of Multi-Racial Comprehensives*, London: Policy Studies Institute.

Smyth, E. 1999, *Do Schools Differ? Academic and Personal Development among Pupils in the Second-Level Sector*, Dublin: Oak Tree Press/ESRI.

Smyth, E. and Hannan, C. 2002, *Who Chooses Science?*, Dublin: The Liffey Press/ESRI.

Smyth, E., McCoy, S., Darmody, M., 2004, *Moving Up. The experiences of first-year students in post-primary education*, Dublin: The Liffey Press/ESRI.

Tashakorri, A. and Teddlie, C., 2003, *Handbook of Mixed Methods in Social and Behavioral Research*, California: Sage.

Teddlie, C. and Stringfield, S. 1993, *Schools Make A Difference: Lessons Learned from a 10-Year Study of School Effects*, New York: Teachers College Press.

Thomas, S., Smees, R., Macbeath, J., Robertson, P., and Demetriou, H. 2000, "Valuing Pupils' Views in Scottish Schools", *Educational Research and Evaluation*, vol. 6, no. 4, pp. 281-316.

Urdan, T. C. Midgley, C. and Wood C. 1995, "Special issues in reforming middle level schools", *Journal of Early Adolescence*, vol. 15, no. 1, pp. 9-37.

Wallace, J. and Wildy, H. (1996) "Old Questions for New Schools: What are the students doing?" Paper presented at AERA Annual Conference, New York. (http://www.ed.uiuc.edu/tta/eval.conf.AERA.html)

Wenz-Gross, M., and Siperstein, G. N. (1998). "Students with Learning Problems at Risk in Middle School: Stress, Social Support, and Adjustment", *Exceptional Children*, vol. 65, no. 1. (Retrieved March 11, 2005, from Questia database, http://www.questia.com)

Willis, P. 1977, *Learning to Labour: How working-class kids get working-class jobs*, Farnborough: Saxon House.